IDEALS AND REALITIES
OF
Ph.D. ADVISING

Intercontinental Series in Sociology

Advisory Editors: Don Martindale and Joseph S. Roucek
Series Editor: Raj P. Mohan

IDEALS AND REALITIES
OF
Ph.D. ADVISING

By

Don Martindale

Intercontinental Series in Sociology No. 3

INTERCONTINENTAL PRESS, PUBLISHERS
Ghaziabad (U.P.) India

World Copyrights Controlled by
Intercontinental Press, Publishers

First Published 1980

All rights reserved. No part of this publication may be reproduced, stored in a retrieval system, or transmitted, in any form or by any means, electronic, mechanical, photocopying, recording or otherwise, without the prior permission of the copyright owner.

ISBN 0-933142-02-1

Published by
Intercontinental Press, Publishers
P. O. Box 114
Ghaziabad (U.P.) India

ACKNOWLEDGEMENTS

This monograph would not have been possible without the hundred or so doctoral candidates who at one time or other advised with me. I marvel at the world of richness they comprise: the humble and the arrogant, the loyal and the treacherous, the timid and the bold, the straightforward and the tricky. My life has been immeasurably enriched by their tragedies and triumphs, their tears and their laughter. I would not change one of them, including those who found me impossibly deficient from their point of view and from the standpoint of their needs. Against the backdrop of those with whom an advisor fails as well as those with whom he succeeds, he finds the measure of himself. In the fullest sense this monograph is their book.

I also owe a special debt of gratitude to Mrs. Helen Keefe, who worked with so many of their texts, quietly corrected them and put them into final form, and to Edith Martindale who over the years must have brewed a hundred barrels of coffee and baked a ton of cookies and prepared a thousand meals that were served to graduate students during their conferences over their problems and dissertations. This monograph is dedicated to them for they provided the foundation of professional skills, sympathetic understanding and common sense so essential to keep the advising relationship in perspective.

TABLE OF CONTENTS

	Page
PREFACE	
ACKNOWLEDGEMENTS	
LIST OF TABLES	

Chapter

I.	ON ADVISORS	2
II.	ON ADVISEES	27
III.	ADVENTURES IN GRADUATE STUDENT ADVISING	53
IV.	TRANSFERS, DROPOUTS AND FAILURES	86
V.	EX-ADVISEES AS COLLEAGUES	102
VI.	ON BEING REVIEWED BY A FOMER ADVISEE	119
VII.	WAYSIDE ADVENTURES	136
VIII.	ON MALE ADVISORS AND FEMALE ADVISEES	161

Appendix: Statistics on Doctoral Advising in Sociology at Minnesota	187
Bibliography	198
INDEX	204

For

Edith Martindale and Helen Keefe

PREFACE

Aspirations for advanced degrees have played an ever expanding role in American higher education during the course of the twentieth century. In the late nineteenth century the Ph. D. was introduced into American higher education after the model of the German research degree in the natural sciences. In 1900 only 400 Ph.D.'s were being granted yearly in American universities. However, the Ph.D. was being institutionalized and emerging as the criterion of respectability in all areas of learning. College presidents began to vie with one another to increase the number of Ph.D.'s on their staffs. By 1960 American colleges and universities were granting 10,000 Ph.D.'s a year and the demand was escalating. By 1968–1969, 250 graduate schools in the United States were offering the Ph.D. The rise of the Ph.D. was closely correlated with other trends in American higher education such as departmentalization, bureaucratization, professionalism and emphasis upon research. Between 1950 and 1970 the percentage of faculty with doctoral degrees in institutions of higher learning of all types in the United States had increased from 37 to 50 percent. By 1975 the number of Ph.D.'s granted yearly in the United States was around 36,000. The number was estimated to reach 43,000 yearly by 1985. Sixty-six earned doctoral degrees were awarded in sociology in 1947–1948; in 1973–1974, 632 doctoral degrees were awarded. And in 1975 in the 50 United States and its outlying parts 401 institutions of higher learning were offering the doctoral degree, 115 offered the Ph.D. in sociology, an additional 94 offered the M. A. or M. S. only.

PREFACE

With the emergence of the Ph.D. program in American education in the late nineteenth century and its institutionalization in the early twentieth, a new type of student appeared. The Ph.D. candidate was older, more knowledgeable and more mature than the undergraduate. With his appearance came a new function of higher education: not simply to transmit culture across the generations, but to create, to add to the body of knowledge. The professor's role was transformed in the process, for his task was not to inspire respect for the old, but to become an agent of change, to assist his graduate student advisees in revising and expanding intellectual culture. And while he primarily met the undergraduates in group situations, when the professor advised his graduate students in the last and almost important phases of their doctorates, their dissertations, the average doctoral advisor (some advisors confine their relationships to the signing of forms and chairing committees) entered into a prolonged one-on-one student-teacher relationship that was inevitably more private, intimate and personal than any other form of teaching.

Although there have been many studies of higher education in general and the doctoral degree in particular, and although it is often observed that the Ph.D. advisor-advisee relationship is unusually sensitive and important, and while there have been occasional surveys of the attitudes of doctoral candidates toward their sponsors, the relationship has rarely been isolated for special study in its own right.

Even the contrast between two discrete types of doctoral advising relationship has been unstudied: the advisor voluntarily chosen by the advisee; the advisee appointed by the professor. The appointed advisee has largely been a phenomenon of the physical sciences where professors have ongoing research projects. Much of the time, the projects on which advisees work provide them with financial

PREFACE

support and with data for their dissertations. Meanwhile they learn through apprenticeship how to conduct research. Their findings often form a subphase of those of the project as a whole. It is usually taken for granted that fiindings by the student are to be jointly published with the project director as senior author. However, when the Ph. D. migrated to the social sciences and the humanities, the graduate student had fewer opportunities to work on the projects of his advisor. In a situation where the advisee had to invent his own project and gather his own data, it was inevitable he also should claim the right to choose his own advisor. In this case his advisor faced the dilemma of how much help and advice he should put into an advisee's problem, for the student was inclined to view his findings and any publication that resulted from them as his exclusive property, no matter how much help he had obtained. If there is an advance risk of exploitation: the appointed advisee runs the greater risk of exploitation by the professor; the voluntarily chosen advisor runs the greater risk of exploitation by the student. This is a hypothesis that deserves further study.

As funded research has become increasingly available in the social sciences and the humanities, the appointed advisee has made his appearance in these spheres beside the voluntary advisee. The contrasting norms of the two types of advising, on occasion, has had anomalous consequences which are little understood and the problem of who is exploiting whom has become more complex.

Inevitably in an area where the stakes are so high, the antagonists so nearly equal, and objective studies so few, in institutions of higher learning with doctoral programs gossip about the doctoral advisory relationship is perennial. Even when I was still an undergraduate at the University of Wisconsin, I recall my excitement, when Alexander Goldenweiser, who had befriended me, explained how Ruth Benedict had come into his classes as a poetees (with training in English) at a time her marriage was breaking up. He had, he said, read her poetry and had become convinced that she had the ideal talents and background for pursuit of the concept of cultural configurationism, an idea which Goldenweiser himself had developed as a major solution to the controversy ever totemism and as a resolution of the problem of where to draw the line between cultural creativity and diffusionism. I gathered that, in large measure, *Patterns of Culture* had been a product of Gouldenwiser's advice. I do not know whether Goldenweiser's personal tragedy forced him to leave Columbia before or after Benedict's completion of her degree, but it was clear that he had played a major role in what was to become her distinctive contribution to anthropology. As a result, I was intrigued by ambivalent attitudes toward Goldenweiser that appeared whenever Benedict had reference to him in her later work. Somewhere there had been a fascinating, but unexplored advisor-advisee relaship between them.

Again, I recall the cocktail party in the early 1940s, shortly after I had begun my own graduate work and the amusement that greeted the story by a young English professor of her encounter with the great anthropologist Bronislaw Malinowski. They had met on shipboard either on the way to or from England. Malinowski gallantly suggested that she abandon her degree plans in English literature and major with him in anthropology, and urged they initiate the new relationship by a visit to his cabin for an adventure between the sheets. Malinowski's generous offer, she said, was declined.

Years later, a visiting English anthropologist and I were talking about Malinowski. He said that every one of Malinowski's advisees, in the end, became bitter enemies with him. While Malinowski was brilliant, he explained, he tried

PREFACE

to dominate his advisees the rest of their lives, leaving them no choice, if they wished professional autonomy of their own, other than to break with him.

I have no way of knowing how much of Goldenweiser's stories about Benedict and the tales of Malinowski's role as a would-be and actual advisor are true. They are one-sided and fragmentary. However, they typify the endless lore that circulates institutions of higher learning about the doctoral advising activities of the great and the not so great. Both the fascination of such tales and the lack of empirical studies in depth led me to undertake the present monograph on the sociology of academic advising.

Between 1948, when I completed my Ph.D. and became qualified to serve as a graduate advisor, and the summer of 1977 I guided a total of 73 individuals through the Ph.D. degree. Along the way I also had many M. A. candidates, but I decided, in the present study, to concentrate on doctoral candidates. During the same period around 30 additional persons either voluntarily left me for other advisors, or were rejected and chose other advisors, or stayed with me but drifted away from sociology, or failed to negotiate the obstacles of the Ph.D. The present monograph is based on a sample of 100 Ph.D. candidates of which three fourth successfully completed the degree with me.

The study is based on only one type of advisor-advisee relationship: that in which the advisee voluntarily chooses his advisor. Whenever an advisor is pursuing research of his own with funding he has secured and on which he is offering a student an opportunity for support and training, the appointed advisee is inevitable. The problems of the appointed advisee are necessarily somewhat different from those of the voluntary advisee. Since I have not had direct experience with appointed advisees the present account does not explore their problems in depth.

PREFACE

Other limitations of this study flow from its character as a personal document based on participant observation. I have tried to avoid self-serving or self-justifying formulations, but it is hard to determine when one has succeeded. In all instances where individuals might be hurt or embarrassed by the account names have been altered for their protection.

Don Martindale
June 1978

CHAPTER 1

ON ADVISORS

It is a familiar stereotype that a student is often socialized through identification with a teacher. The argument has been advanced that identification with his doctoral advisor is a primary device by which the graduate student is socialized into the profession.[1] And while it appears to be true that some graduate students do take over characteristics of their advisors when they are accepted and encouraged, 26 percent of the graduate students queried in one study indicated that given another opportunity they would choose a different advisor.[2]

On every campus professors acquire reputations as good and bad, indifferent and fascinating. Joseph Adelson opined that the large number of college teachers are good in the sense that they are lucid, articulate, and fair. But also he is quite correct in his observation that while students often learn much from them, most teachers do not make much difference in the students' lives apart from the specific learning these teachers impart. Some teachers, however, lift the student to a new plane.

I think now of a former colleague of mine, in some ways a truly great man, who is so ebullient, erratic, and distractible, so easily carried away by the rocketing course of his thought, that his students—even the bright ones—just sit there, benumbed, bewildered—and finally enthralled. They know themselves to be close to a presence, and are willing to suffer incoherence to join vicariously in that demonic enthusiasm.[3]

Borrowing from a typology of healers (the shaman, the magician, the priest, the mystic healer, and the naturalistic-physician) developed by anthropologist Merrill

Jackson, Adelson isolated three types of teachers he thought capable of transforming students in their basic sense: the teacher as shaman; the teacher as priest; and the teacher as mystic healer. The shaman teacher, he urges, may be withdrawn, diffident and humble, but he keeps his audience's attention focused on himself and invites his students to observe his personality in its encounter with subject matter. "He stresses charm, skill, manna, in the self's entanglement with ideas. When this orientation is combined with unusual gifts, we have a charismatic teacher."[4] The priestly teacher "stresses not his personal virtues, but his membership in a powerful or admirable collectivity, e. g., physics, psychoanalysis, classical scholarship...The priestly teacher says: 'I am valuable for what I belong to. I represent and personify a collective identity.' "[5] The teacher as mystic healer, according to Adelson, is altruistic. "He concentrates neither on himself, nor the subject matter, nor the discipline, but on the student, saying; 'I will help you become what you are.' We may recall Michelangelo's approach to sculpture; looking at the raw block of marble, he tried to uncover the statue within it. So does the altruistic teacher regard his unformed student; this type of teacher keeps his own achievement and personality secondary; he works to help the student find what is best and most essential within himself."[6]

Among teachers there are also, antimodels and disappointing models. "Here the student uses teacher as a lodestar, from which he sails away as rapidly as he can, seeming to say: Whatever he is, I will not be; whatever he is for, I will be against. Teachers who exercise this power of revulsion are, in their own way, charismatic types: indeed, the teacher who is charismatically positive for some will be negative for other. He breeds disciples or enemies; few remain unmoved. If we follow a student's development closely enough we generally discover both positive and negative models; the decision to be or become like someone goes hand in hand with a negative choice of identity and ideal."[7] Distinct from the antimodel, in Adelson's view, is the disappointing model, a former positive model in which the student finds some imperfection or fatal flaw. Sometimes Adelson argues a student undertakes a relentless search for an adequate model, successively idealizing one model after another only to be plunged into disappointment as he finds in the model some human frailty, especially lack of moral perfection, integrity, fairness, ethical sensitivity, or courage.

Adelson's models of outstanding teachers are, of course, speculative, although anyone who has spent some time around an institution of higher learning will recognize the types of phenomena he describes. Furthermore, by his own admission the large mujority of teachers, while good, are not outstanding. And Adelson was describing teachers rather than advisors, but then every academic advisor is first a teacher. Nevertheless, this typology of teachers begins the isolation of differences between advisors which must be taken into account before advisee reactions to them can be evaluated. Before the statistical study of the advisor-advisee relationship can become fruitful, qualitative studies of concrete cases are desirable. However, the sociology of doctoral advising is not an intensively cultivated area of the profession at either a qualitative or quantitative level. Most individuals who have earned the Ph.D. have had only three or four academic advisors during the course of their student careers. This is a small sample to begin with and since a given advisor is usually confined to a single phase of the student's career (junior college, senior college, graduate school) comparison between advisors is untrustworthy. Nevertheless advisors do acquire reputations of being good, bad, tricky, unreliable, or exploitive, including sexually exploitive. However, such reputations can be inaccurate. One individual who earned the Ph.D. under my direction reported after it was all over: "When I first started to major with you I heard perfectly awful things about you. Not a single one was true." I did not ask him why he had decided, despite this, to major with me. Another individual reported after the completion of her degree, "It is ironic. They said you were a theorist without the slightest conception of methods. I took all the courses in methods and statistics the department had to offer, but it was you who showed me how to put them all together " I did not ask her who "they" were for I assumed she was reporting the gossip of other faculty and students. When the sociology of advising is eventually brought under full examination, the problem of how reputations are acquired and lost and when they are deserved and when not, will need to be examined. The present informal essay reviews the two sides of the advising process primarily from the standpoint of my own experience.

In the seven years of course work at the University of Wisconsin, Madison, from the status of freshman to the completion of Ph.D. work, interrupted by four years in the Army of the United States during World War II, I had a total of four advisors: in my first two years while I was in classical humanities, I had Walter Agard, a fine classicist, as an advisor; after shifting to philosophy, in which, during the next three years, I earned the B.A. and M.A., my advisor was Eliseo Vivas; after the M. A. when, in 1940, I shifted to sociology I chose as an advisor the theorist of the department, Howard P. Becker resuming work with him again after four years of war service (1942-1946). Since Becker was away in Europe as Chief of Higher Education in the American Zone of Germany during the time I was trying to complete a dissertation (in 1947) and, since I was having difficulty conferring with him, I obtained permission from the department head, T. C. McCormick, and the administration of the graduate school to change advisors to Hans Gerth with whom I completed the Ph.D.

The personalities of my advisors were very different and the problems I faced with each were distinct. Professor Agard appeared anxious to provide a lower division student in the classical humanities with the soundest and most thorough background possible. I was working my way through school and seeking both to arrange a schedule with work time and to take a full program. I found him helpful and understanding. However, the classical curriculum was quite time-consuming. Professor Laird[8] of the classics department, for example, was an old-fashioned task master and did not hesitate to assign thirty pages of Greek text three times a week, expecting complete mastery of each assignment. This meant a minimum of five hours a day on Greek alone and, with another language, science, and mathematics to get up at the same time, there were not enough hours in a day to keep up with course work and make a living during the depths of the Depression. Over and beyond this I was finding no time left over from the study of classical antiquity to pursue other intellectual interests. When I made an appointment with Professor Agard to explain my decision to shift majors to philosophy, he was deeply shocked.

"One shifts from the classics when one is failing, not when one is running a straight A average," he protested. He then tried to persuade me to make a formal complaint to the dean of the arts college. (It was not until much later, that I learned that Agard had been brought to the Wisconsin campus by Glenn Frank to participate in Wisconsin's famous Experimental College), and there was tension between Frank's appointees and some of the older traditional faculty.)[9] However, I refused to do this, explaining that while I remained fascinated by classical antiquity, I was also interested in the general history of western thought and that I intended to shift fields anyway and not simply because of the time demands of the classical curriculm. With some regrets I left Agard for a new advisor.

Eliseo Vivas, a small, olive-skinned Latin American with straight black hair, a round face and darting brown eyes, was temperamental, given to sharp alterations of mood, with a charming accent and mannerism that endeared him to the students. He had a dazzling style of lecturing and an interest in art, literature and aesthetics. He was, unquestionably, one of the most popular instructors at the University of Wisconsin during the 1930s, although he also aroused intense antagonism in a small minority of the students. His moods tended to alternate between euphoria and despair. He was magnetically self-centered and one quickly learned that an advisee's problems, program or progress had virtually no existence for him. He had a fascinating way of pouring out a torrent of complaints against what he viewed as the latest machiavellian machinations of the Philosophy Department Chairman, Max Otto. In a section from a "quasi-biography" in which he calls himself "Alonzo Quijada" and he calls Otto "Maximilian Klotz," still, in retirement, Vivas speaks of Otto in terms similar to those he employed when discussing him with advisees in the 1930s.

> Upon his return to State Alonzo became the assistant of Professor Maximilian Klotz, one of the most popular teachers of the university.

> A superb speaker, he employed superior rhetorical powers in dishing out the thin gruel that he took to be philosophic wisdom—relativism and atheism....From the relativism he preached some students naturally inferred that the girls of State should come of age in the same

way as those of Samoa and that they, the boys, were the ones to help the girls grow up.

That students should interpret Maxie Waxie's teaching in this manner was, in one sense, very incongruous, for his relativism was never intended to reach Samoa or cannibalism. The man who had shed his blue uniform, his tambourine, and Christ, and had put William James and John Dewey in Christ's place, had not rid himself of sexual prudishness, in spite of the rumors Alonzo had occasionally heard of a "friendship" before his marriage with a male French teacher who had left State, long before Alonzo arrived, for an eastern university.[10]

To an undergraduate student in a major midwestern university at a time when the American universities were much more rigidly stratified than they have been since the late sixties' counter-cultural revolt, the frank criticism of his colleagues and departmental superiors by Vivas was heady stuff. In the imagery of the classical humanities which I had left for philosophy, it was like an ordinary mortal being given a ringside seat to witness the conflicts of the gods on Olympus.

At the time (the late 1930s) Vivas was closely identified with such staunch liberals as Sidney Hook with whom he was personal friends. Vivas was in fact to describe his intellectual evolution from that period to the present as a movement "from a confused and domestic liberalism," through "fellow-travelling demi-Marxism," to conservatism.[11]

Many of the liberals, including Vivas, reacted strongly against educational ideals and programs centering on the one-hundred great books sponsored by Robert Hutchins and Mortimer Adler at the University of Chicago. This program was subjected to devastating criticism in Vivas's classes. Hence, when Adler was invited to give an evening lecture on the Wisconsin campus, many of Vivas students attended to see the "fireworks." Vivas attended, sat in the front row during the lecture, but said nothing. I was personally relieved. I thought it was bad taste for a faculty member to heckle a visiting scholar in public (and, in any case, I thought it inappropriate to create an ugly scene) and despite the popular tendency in liberal and radical circles to attack the great-books enthusiasts, I was enamoured of the classics my private study of the classes had sent me into classical humanities in the first place. In his lecture incidentally, Mortimer Adler acquitted himself well.

The next morning a brilliant Irish student colleague who had always been ambivalent about Vivas approached me in the Rathskeller. "I see your mentor, Vivas, was at Adler's talk last night," he observed, and, with heavy sarcasm, "He didn't say a word. I think he's a coward, what do you think?"

I knew that some students had expected Vivas to challange Adler. "Maybe you're right and maybe not," I said. "I have no way of knowing his motives, but I can see nothing wrong in his keeping his counsel rather than harassing a visiting speaker."

Later that day, to my horror, I heard that the student was reporting widely over the campus, that I had said that Vivas was silent at the Adler speech out of cowardice. In my confusion and embarrassment, I could think of no way to clarify the situation other than to tell Vivas about the entire incident myself, rather than to permit it to come to his attention, as it was most certain to do, in the normal course of affairs. Vivas took my report of the incident with apparent calm.

However, later I heard that Vivas had an angry exchange with the student in the basement of the library during which the student admitted he was the author of the rumor. When I came to my rooming house, my landlady was waiting for me with a letter from Vivas and the report that he had called urgently several times to ask that it be returned to him unopened. This I did. Finally, Vivas arranged a meeting with me. He stated that he was going to talk to me like a "Dutch Uncle" and proceeded to lecture me on my shortcomings for about two hours. I was unable to determine quite what it was I had done wrong. Once this storm passed, he returned to one of his enchanting sunshine moods. As far as I could tell, my indiscretion had been to be the messenger of ugly gossip. However, under the circumstance I could not see that I had any other choice. But then as Lawrence Stern had observed, when a man is trapped between two indiscretions, society will blame him whichever one he chooses.

The year I earned the M. A. in philosophy, Vivas was away on a research fellowship. I was told by a member of the University Awards Committee what had happened to my fellowship application for the following year. I had been recommended by Max Otto, Chairman of the Philosophy Department for a small fellowship that paid $400 a year, a fellowship which was traditionally assigned to promising foreign students. Meanwhile, Otto had recommended a graduate student from Iowa for an All-University Fellowship which was open to competition by all students internal or external to the university and which paid $600 a year. The committee removed my name from the first fellowship on the grounds that it was an inappropriate nomination. However, they thought my credentials were superior to the Iowa student and hence awarded the All-University Fellowship to me. When Otto heard of the committee's action, it was reported, he was furious and insisted that the committee either give him what he had asked for or nothing. The committee rose to the occasion, and replied, "All right, you get nothing."

When Vivas returned to the campus and I related the incident, he stated. "You were being discriminated against because of me." As an after thought he added, "Thank God, I was not on campus when this happened. I might have been tempted to defend you and I can't afford it."[12] This was stated with such complete unselfconsciousness that for the first time I realized that the affairs of advisees were as remote from Vivas as the stars.[13]

While the reaction of my advisor to the events of my lost fellowship came as a shock and was the final confirming event in my decision to transfer to sociology I did not doubt for a moment that he was correct and could not be expected to hurt himself by helping me. But it also left no doubt that I did not belong in a field where my advisor did not dare come to my rescue.

When I rationalized my decision later to leave philosophy I reasoned that perhaps things had worked out for the best. For if I had hope of support, I might have been tempted to stay on in philosophy to my ultimate sorrow. As it was I had the opportunity to undertake work in an entirely new field, but with the advantage of extensive experience in two previous fields to draw upon. Furthermore, I had learned a most important lesson: when a crisis came in a university one could depend only upon one's self. For the rest one has to learn to work with people as they are and not to impose expectations on them they will not and cannot fulfill.

I still remember with delight all the enchanting mannerisms, the ingenious attention-gathering tricks, the dazzling alteration of emotional light and shadow, the egocentric conceits, the play with his audience as proverbial sayings were deliberately flubbed—providing students both with the insight yielded by an appropriate quotation and the pleasure of correcting, in their own minds, the professor—with which Vivas used to fascinate the students during those innocent days long ago when all was youth and youth was hope.

A problem that had repeatedly occurred to me during my years in philosophy was why equally plausible philosophic systems remained unexplored until, it seemed, the times were ripe for them. There were problems that could not be solved by the study of thought-systems alone. Moreover, a residual effect of my time in classical humanities was the realization that at times society and culture, including thought systems, were closely interrelated. The promise of sociology and of social theory was twofold: concentration on the theoretical explanations of society and on the role of society in the shaping of thought. These were empirical problems that could not be solved by philosophical analysis alone. It was not clear to me then, nor is it now, whether my increasing conviction that a rocky road lay ahead in philosophy at Wisconsin (because of disapproval of me by Otto as an advisee of Vivas and the inability of Vivas to defend me) was a major component in this shift of intellectual emphasis. In any case Howard P. Becker of the sociology department had been the man on the university fellowship committee who had informed me of the committee's action in awarding me a fellowship and of Otto's peevish response to it. I turned to him as my advisor in my new field of sociology.

In 1940, when I first met him, Howard P. Becker looked like a winner. He was forty years old; he had translated Leopold von Wiese from German; he had co-authored, with Harry Elmer Barnes, *Social Thought From Lore to*

Science, the best history of social thought to appear to that date. Becker had been raised by his Scotch grandparents in Canada and had worked his way through college, becoming a machine designer for International Harvester. He was lean and vigorous and reported to practice boxing in his basement. He had a brilliant speaking voice and a confident style of delivery which made him a popular lecturer. He had an excellent memory and on appropriate occasions often quoted from *Alice in Wonderland.* Before Christmas he read passages from Kenneth Grahame's *The Wind in the Willows* to the delight of his classes. Rumor had it that Becker was to be the next chairman of the sociology department and the next president of the American Sociological Society. A large number of the most promising graduate students including C. Wright Mills, in sociology at Wisconsin (which was rated as the third best department in the country) were majoring with Becker.

Disillusionment came quickly in sociology. After the discipline of classical humanities and philosophy, sociology was easy. In Gerth's seminars I often found other students asking me to explain what Gerth meant. However, shortly after entering sociology full-time and taking four courses, I received four B's in a single semester. Students around me who had turned to me for help received A's. I was thunderstruck. Then to my complete astonishment three of the four professors, including Hans Gerth and Howard Becker, my new advisor, explained to me that although my work was excellent they had given me B's because at a special department meeting there had been complaint that they had been giving out too many A's. All three professors explained that they had given me B's because, in view of my general record, "I could take it." They had, in short, rewarded work which they told me privately was excellent by giving me the worst semester's record I had ever received in six years work at the

University of Wisconsin starting as a freshman. Whatever problems classical humanities and philosophy had presented, its professors had recognized merit and had rewarded it. What kind of field and advisor had I chosen, that admittedly downgraded excellence and graded on the basis of favoritism? I was disturbed ot the thought of what would happen if I had to apply to another university and present a record which was crumbling into mediocrity. However, by this time war was looming on the horizon. There seemed to be only one reasonable course of action, to wind up my degree work with all possible speed. If one remained as a student in a university long enough, disaster appeared to be inevitable. In talking to C. Wright Mills about our mutual advisor, Mills, who had been having increasing difficulty with Becker, dismissed him contemptuously as a "mere editor."

I took a heavy schedule of classes to wind up my course requirements as soon as possible. I wrote off my two languages, French and German, and took the special examination the sociology department required in the history of social thought. I checked with Becker to see what he had in mind for a Ph.D. thesis.

Becker said that he wished me to do a thesis on the stranger. This was an amorphous suggestion, for who has not been a stranger somewhere some time? Becker did not say, as I was to discover later, that he had recently read and had been impressed by Simmel's essay on "The Stranger." Had he done so, it would have helped defining a problem and formulating a theory. Moreover, at the time there was no course in methodology to say nothing of thesis writing—in the sociology department of the University of Wisconsin. T. C. McCormick was a good statistician, but a poor teacher. Becker, when pressed on methodology, always had recourse to the "constructed type," but it was not possible to formulate a systematic procedure in its employment from his particular formulations of it. (Becker made no reference to Weber's methodological writings which did not appear in translation until 1949.) At the time Becker treated the ideal type as if it were the end point of research rather than a beginning.

Nevertheless, without advice, suggestions or models to work from for a thesis on the stranger I pursued my explorations and note taking among the almost endlessly conceivable varieties of "strangeness" with the idea of locating a limited number of forms or types for comparative study. However, I became eligible for the draft before I was able to take my preliminary examinations and my local draft board was unsympathetic to an extension of time to permit me to take them. My graduate work was interrupted by four years of military service during World War II.

When I returned to the campus after military service, I was struck by the transformation in Becker's image among the graduate students. To be sure, immediately before the war, Becker's hopes had been thwarted on a number of fronts: the sociology department had passed him over and had awarded the chairmanship to T. C. McCormick, an old graduate students rival from Chicago days (Becker had advised with Robert Park; McCormick with William Ogburn). Moreover, the rumor that Becker was in line for presidency of the national society proved to be false. Still, despite the skepticism about Becker as an advisor by Mills most of the better graduate students of the department before the war were majoring with Becker.

After the war all this had changed. Disillusionment with Becker was universal. There were numerous complaints of his irascibility and of his exploitation of the students. Becker himself, who had served in the Office of Strategic Services during the war, was alternately defensive and aggressive and appeared to be determined to spend as much time off the campus and in goverment service as possible. However, upon my return to the campus I was too busy completing my own work to worry about these changes. I restudied for, took, and passed the preliminary examinations. I began teaching sociology on the University of Wisconsin extension circuit only to be called into residence at Madison at the end of the first semester, to take over Becker's courses while he left to become Chief of Higher Education in the American zone of occupied Germany.

As soon as my preliminary examinations were out of the way, I had explored with Becker the prospects for a new Ph.D. topic, for during the war years the extensive work toward a dissertation on the stranger had long since gone down the drain. Meanwhile I had thought about the problem of an eventual dissertation many times during military service. I had come to the conclusion that, if possible, a dissertation should be based on first-hand research or at least first-hand experience. Nothing could take the place of full acquaintance with the facts to be accounted for. With this in mind I had tried to keep my eyes open and to make full field notes of my military experience, which could be written down in my letters and retained for analysis after the war. It was not possible for me to attempt a statistical study of some phase of military life at the time, hence my materials could only consist of field notes as a participant observer. Meanwhile I had thought much about possible ways of transforming the ideal type into an instrument of research, rather than leaving it in the form of a pithy summary after the fact of what one had learned.

It seemed to me that ideal types acquired the property of investigative tools when they were formulated during preliminary research as tentative estimates of the contrasting properties of comparative situations. In the case of a wartime army, for example, there were at least two major types of soldiers: professionals who view the military as a career and civilian soldiers, drafted for the duration plus six months. Moreover, a major problem for wartime armies is the maintenance of morale. If there was, in fact, a basic difference, between these two types of soldiers, the problem of morale should assume different forms for each. Moreover, since morale, whether it be of civilian soldiers or professionals, is also affected by situational factors, some contrasts should appear between circumstances where individuals are able to do virtually nothing about their circumstances except wait, as in replacement depots or on troop ships, and the intensively active occasions of combat. It should be possible, thus, to explore the problem of morale in terms of crudely indicated contrasts between types of military personnel (civilian soldiers and professionals) and types of situations (periods of forced inactivity and periods of combat).

When I approached Becker to propose a new dissertation topic, he had, meanwhile, become enthusiastic about the Hawthorn Electric Studies of Roethlisberger and Dickson and indicated he wished me to undertake a dissertation on the sociology of work. When I explained that I wished to study some problems of military morale during wartime and had gathered field notes for such a study, he accepted the idea without objection. And when I brought in my field notes for review he was so impressed by them that he approached Mark H. Ingraham, dean of the college of letters and science at Wisconsin, who authorized $250 out of dean's funds to have my notes typed and bound and placed in the university archives. However, Becker soon left for his overseas assignment, leaving me to teach his courses and to struggle ahead on the dissertation in whatever spare time I could find.

I soon became aware of a new hazard on the road to the Ph.D. in sociology at Wisconsin which had not been present before the war. No student proposing a thesis topic at Wisconsin was permitted to begin his dissertation until he had presented his proposal before an evening meeting of the entire sociology faculty. As a member of the faculty I was invited to attend these sessions. They quickly proved to be agonizing ordeals for the candidates. A candidate read his proposal. A brief period of silence followed, broken first by polite rather miscellaneous questions. Gradually the tone of the questions became more serious. Eventually the criticism became devastating. The rule was that no faculty member questioned another, but what one professor did not object to, some other one did. Proposals were quickly torn to ribbons and the faces of the victims sometimes turned alternately red and pale. In some instances anxiety was so intense that sweat rolled down the cheeks of the victims and dripped from their chins. No candidate who ran this gauntlet ever managed to complete a dissertation. Graduate students began to leave Madison for other schools. Eventually T. C. McCormick called a special meeting of the faculty: "Let's face it," he said, "the procedure is a disaster." By vote of the faculty it was abandoned.

When I asked Gerth where this system of forcing all candidates to run the gauntlet of the entire faculty before being permitted to undertake their dissertation had come from, he related the following tale. Becker had put a candidate to work on the task of studying *gemeinschaft* among Russian, Polish and German peasants Unfortunately the candidate was unable to read any of the languages, although much of the most important material was untranslated. Gerth who was on the committee -was acquainted with the relevant literature in German and Selig Perlman, who was also on the committee, read Russian, Polish, and German and was familiar with source materials in all three languages. Both scholars recommended that the dissertation not be undertaken since the primary literature was inaccessible to the candidate. However, the candidate informed Perlman and Gerth that Becker had insisted that he keep the topic. Gerth and Perlman then threw up their hands, but gave the candidate what they considered to be the minimum literature in English and resigned themselves to the prospect of a relatively inadequate piece of work.

When Becker brought the candidate up for his final oral, Perlman and Gerth discovered that, although the recommended literature was in the bibliography it had not been read and covered in the dissertation. With this revelation their questioning of the candidate assumed an increasingly serious tone. However, instead of defending his candidate who had acted on his advice, Becker turned on him. Perlman and Gerth were so dismayed by this turn of affairs, they passed the candidate as a victim of his advisor's poor advice. However, after the examination Perlman wrote McCormick a letter stating that he was unwilling to sit on the examining committees of any more candidates of the sociology department of the University of Wisconsin. It was this correspondence that led to the institution of evening meetings by the entire faculty to review every thesis proposal.

It was not this story nor even the prospects of running the gauntlet of the evening thesis examination by the faculty, however, that led me to change advisors to Hans Gert . Becker, who had gone to Europe for a year, took a further extended leave. Rumor had it, that he might remain in Europe permanently. Meanwhile, I found it impossible to work ahead on the dissertation, for my letters to Becker went unanswered. At the same time, McCormick was pressuring me to complete the degree. I asked Gerth if he was willing to serve as my advisor and when he agreed I approached McCormick with the same request. McCormick enthusiastically approved and intervened to overcome graduate school resistance. Once more I found myself with a new advisor.

The problems presented by Gerth's advising were distinctive. Becker's suggestions were narrow and limited; Gerth's were broad and diffuse. Hans Gerth, who had studied under Karl Mannheim and had worked as a reporter, was part genius, part antiquarian, part traditional German scholar. His mentality was baroque; his inclination was to pursue a theme, not in its major mode, but in its variations. He loved used book stores and spent many hours in them in search of unusual books. Gerth's mastery of the central argument of any given theory often appeared sketchy while his inclination was to pour into the discussion all sorts of odds and ends of esoteric information. He had an unusual ability to put himself into most diverse roles and to explore their significance with astonishing insight. He could not, for long, pursue a single course of thought without digressing to explore fascinating byways until his listener—and sometimes even Gerth himself—was thoroughly confused as to the direction of the argument.

A thesis conference with Gerth was frustrating. If one came to the conference with a problem and some confusion, one often left with additional problems and with one's confusion confounded. Before one could even explain what was on one's mind, Gerth leaped to conclusions, interrupted, and was off and running with fascinating comments, suggestions, sources to check, and digressions about interesting sidelights of the issues as he interpreted them. Instead of a single well-chosen reference to the precise problem one had in mind, one received dozens of references to problems Gerth had in mind. One left such a conference in a state of bewilderment unless one firmly kept in mind the ideas that led to the meeting in the first place and quietly reformulated them after Gerth had finally run out of steam.

After a thesis conference with Gerth I usually had to spend hours clarifying for myself the points of coincidence and difference between what I had been trying to do and what had been cast up during the interview. It was important to check out all suggestions, even though nine out of ten proved to be irrelevant, for the tenth was often invaluable. Besides, if one did not check out everything and was prepared to say why it was not relevant, Gerth had an uncanny way of remembering at the next conference what he had suggested and demanding to know why it had not been checked out.

However, I found that if I stuck by my guns and refused to be distracted from my theme, Gerth's conferences became a testing ground of the argument. Along the way, he often came up with suggestions that were invaluable, though they had to be worked up and polished. His basic methodological advice, to marshall all evidence that supported the thesis, was sound. Within two months after changing advisors I had completed the dissertation in first draft; within six months the dissertation had finally been read and I had passed the final oral.

When I review the sparse literature on graduate advisors in the light of experience with my own advisors, it is incomplete and operates with categories so broad and loose as to leave the matters they are intended to explain undeterminable. Adelson's teacher-typology, shamans, priests, mystics, and antiheroes, do not fit very well. Presumably shaman-advisors are narcissistic egocentrics who nevertheless convey an exemplary preoccupation with knowledge and culture, priest-advisors presumably convey a respect and awe for knowledge and culture for which they are mere spokesmen; mystic-advisors are selfless altruists humbly seeking only the opportunity to evoke the genius of the student. There were no mystics among my advisors. So far as there was an approximation of Adelson's priest type, my first advisor in classical humanities came closest. To me, at least, Agard conveyed the sense that the classical heritage of the West was a tradition of immeasurable worth for which, as a teacher, he was a devoted spokesman. In general most of my advisors—and it was my impression that most of the more dramatic university professors—were prima donnas with strong components of egocentricity which places them in Adelson's category of shaman teachers. However, there were major differences between Vivas, Becker and Gerth which outweighed their similarities. The category shaman-teacher is too crude to be of much use.

I do not recall that I ever viewed any of my advisors as other than human and fallible. As a matter of fact, I and most other students I knew took special delight in their human traits which personalized and endeared them to us. We did not want unapproachable perfection from them. To turn a former advisor into an antihero, was unthinkable: to put one's self in the position where one had to accept the exact opposite of a professor, would be to give him complete—though negative—power over one's mental life. Nevertheless, the point still remains, Adelson's attempt to type teachers opens up an area of inquiry that should be empirically explored.

From time to time, students of graduate education get around to the task of exploring what graduate students think of their teachers and advisors. In one study Ann Heiss[14] interviewed one hundred doctoral students. They were asked what role they felt an advisor should play as he guided them through their programs. She summarized their conclusions as follows; "Essentially, they expected him to be a critic but a constructive counselor, a relentless taskmaster but a supportive colleague, a model of scholarship but an understanding tutor."[15]

To Summarize this contradictory assemblage of dream images by graduate students : the ideal advisor should simultaneously represent the shaman (particularly as an exemplary charismatic), the priest, and the mystic (who devotes his soul power to evoking the genius of the graduate student) all at one and the same time. Adelson has a point after all.

In *The Challenge to the Graduate Schools* Heiss selected for study a sample of the ten most prestigious graduate institutions in the United States including: the University of California, Berkley, Columbia, Cornell, Johns Hopkins, Michigan, North Carolina, Northwestern, Stanford and Wisconsin. Among departments selected for study were three from each of four academic divisions—the humanities, social sciences, biological sciences and physical sciences— English, French, history, mathematics, philosophy, physics, physiology, psychology and sociology. To a questionnaire survey of how they evaluated their dissertation sponsors, more than 2000 graduate students responded: only 28% received less help than they wanted; 67% received help in selecting a dissertation topic; 60% were accepted as junior colleagues.[16]

While the answers given by this sample of doctoral students to questions evaluating their Ph.D. advisors are interesting, the interpretation of these responses remains open for they rest on incompletely comparable situations. There are not only different types of advisors, but differents types of advisor-advisee relationships, moreover, the students were in variable stages in their Ph.D. programs. Finally, the conventions surrounding doctoral training often differ from division to division in a university and even, at times, from department to department. Once again the examination of the doctoral advising relationships in depth becomes desirable.

Notes

1. D. Gottlieb, "Process of Socialization in American Graduate Schools." Unpublished doctoral dissertation, The University of Chicago, 196..
2. Ann M. Heiss, *Challenges to Graduate Schools* (San Francisco: Jossey-Bass 1970), p. 153.
3. Joseph Adelson, "The Teacher as a Model" in Nevitt Sanford, editor, *The American College: A Psychological and Social Interpretation of the Higher Learning* (New York: John Wiley & Sons, 1962), p. 40..
4. Ibid., p. 407.
5. Ibid., p. 409.
6. Ibid., p. 412.
7. Ibid., p. 414.
8. Arthur Laird, who had been brought to the University of Wisconsin by President Charles Kendall Adams to strengthen its program in the classics, specialized in Greek and comparative philology.
9. Soon after Glenn Frank became president of the University of Wisconsin he brought Alexander Mieklejohn, President of Amherst, to the campus to implement his ideas on a new curriculm for liberal education. Miekeljohn had presented his program in the *Century Magazine* which Frank edited before accepting the Wisconsin appointment. The Experimental College was established within the College of Letters and Science with Mickeljohn as director. The Students, all male, lived together in a dormitory and pursued a unified program of studies for two years largely being taught through tutorial methods. Beginning in 1927 four two-year classes passed through the program before it was terminated. Walter Agard was among the conscientious, idealistic faculty members recruited by Miekeljohn from Amherst in 1927. Although the Experimental College had been terminated by the time I came to Wisconsin, tensions between the faculty that had their origin in its relation to the traditional system persisted.
10. Eliseo Vivas, "Teachers and 'Teachers'," in *Modern Age* (Summer 1975), pp. 228-229. As a youth Max Otto had joined the Salvation Army.
11. Ibid , p. 226.

12. When a long-time associate of Vivas heard this story he observed: "I have more confidence in Eliseo than he has in himself. When the occasion arose he would have found the psychological resources to resist the temptation." But this was the cynical observation of an old rival of Vivas. Over the years many examples were to come to my attention of the ancient professorial practice of attacking each other through their respective students. When eventually my turn came to be subject to attack by some of my colleagues through students I was advising, I began to urge those persons who were advising with me to consider selecting other advisors. Also for a time, I refused to accept additional advisees—an action I deemed in their interest—though I was prepared to help them informally. One scholar who was sent elsewhere in this manner, but on whose committeees I served, confessed at the time I wished him goodbye for the last time that for many years he had felt deep hurt and resentment because I had declined to accept him as an advisee.

13. When I found myself without support, I tried to find part-time employment—or at least summer employment—at one of the industrial firms of Madison such as Ray-O-Vac and Oscar Mayer. However, we were still in the Depression and no jobs could be located. I then explored the possibility of borrowing money to complete my graduate work. In the midst of these endeavors I received a call from Max Otto. He offered me a teaching assistantship in philosophy for the next year. I explained that I had decided to shift my major to sociology. When he said that did not matter, I accepted. Someone suggested at the time that when Otto's plan for a fellowship for the Iowa student fell through, he had arranged for a teaching assistantship to gets him anyway, but the Iowa candidate had dropped out of competition. In any case, I was not inclined to look a gift horse in the mouth, but accepted the offer gratefully since it had no strings attached. During the following year when I began work in sociology, I assisted Otto in Logic and Vivas in the Philosophy of Contemporary Literature. I learned much from both scholars in the process.

14. Ann Heiss, "Berkeley Doctoral Students Appraise Their Doctoral Programs," *The Educational Record* (Winter 1967), pp. 30-44.

15. Heiss, *Challanges to Graduate Schools*, pp. 151-152.

16. Ibid., p. 153.

CHAPTER II

ON ADVISEES

During the two years I taught at the University of Wisconsin, Madison (1946-1948), as the temporary stand-in for Becker during his service in occupied Germany, I also took over his advising duties. Since I was trying to complete my own work, I was forced to bring the two sides of the advising relationship into simultaneous perspective.

If an advisor poured his best ideas into the work and projects of an advisee they became the advisee's property. If an advisee expanded, clarified and added new dimensions to suggestions originally advanced, the advisor was in a strategic position to exploit them for his own professional purposes. Even when work resulted in joint publication, the advisor as senior author received primary credit. Merton described this as the Matthew effect in science.[1] However, the temporary merging of professional identities was subject to exploitation by either party.

Since the advisee was in a power-dependent position on the advisor, he was potentially subject to nonacademic forms of exploitation as well. Advisees have been used as errand boys, baby sitters, handymen. Becker administered a personal lesson to me of professional exploitation.

In the first semester of 1946-1947 when I taught introductory sociology on the extension circuit of the University of Wisconsin (in the cities of Rice Lake, Spooner, Ladysmith and New Richmond), I had found myself without a library to work from and had resorted to the device of writing up the background material I required for my lectures. When I was called into residence to take over Becker's courses in his absence, Becker learned about this material and asked permission to review it. He then made an interesting proposal.

Becker explained that some years before he had delivered lectures in introductory sociology over educational radio and had been given the recordings. He had a secretary transcribe them and, as sociology editor for D. C. Heath and Company, had placed himself under contract for an introductory sociology text. However, the transcriptions of his oral lectures had to be rather completely rewritten to make them fit to print. On the basis of his review of my materials, Becker proposed that the contract with D. C. Heath be re-written as a joint project. Since Becker was still my advisor at the time, I was in no position to reject his proposition. In fact, it seemed a great opportunity to publish material that had not been intended for publication.

Becker made no mention of the terms, but when the contract was delivered I discovered that it awarded 12 percent of the royalties to (introductory texts usually called for 15% royalties). Becker and 4 percent to me. Far from seeing any unfairness in this disproportionate arrangement, Becker explained to me that it was acceptable to him inasmuch as he received another 2 percent royalties as editor of the sociology series. In short, Becker expected me to do virtually all of the work while he had negotiated financial arrangements that would give him three fourths of the royalties. I had heard that young scholars often had to accept a certain amount of exploitation when they first got started in the profession; this, I reasoned, was a case in point.

The arrangement over the joint text dramatized to me the importance of completing the degree before there were other one-sided contracts. I eventually did transfer to Gerth. I received an offer from the University of Minnesota which Wisconsin declined to meet, and accepted the job beginning the fall quarter of 1948. Meanwhile, however, in my spare time I continued to work on the introductory text. Sometime after my transfer to Minnesota when Becker had returned to his teaching duties at Wisconsin (during 1950) I received a letter from Becker informing me that he had changed his mind about joint authoring an introductory text. He explained that he felt that it was professionally essential that he complete the entire volume by himself. He stated that he wanted me to sign a statement agreeing not to write a competing introductory text for 20 years. He proposed to recompense me by offering me a new contract as editor of the Heath sociology series to do a book entirely by myself on social problems.

I realized that Becker was unaware of the fact that I had completed the Ph.D. in his absence, for in the address on the envelope he had written "Mr. Don Martindale," while in his return address he had written "Dr. Howard Becker." I read this as an unsubtle reminder and a threat. This slight of hand over terms of address seemed to say: "Look, son, you had better go along with this arrangement peacefully if you expect to complete the degree." Had I not completed the Ph.D. I would have had no choice but to see all my work on the introductory text disappear under Becker's signature. If I had signed the proposed contract, moreover, I would have been unable to write an introductory sociology text until 1970. As it was, I simply sent Becker's letter on to D. C. Heath and requested that they void the contract, but declined to sign away my rights to the publication of my own material.[2]

When I was hired by Minnesota I had completed the Ph D., hence, shortly after joining the department I was appointed to the graduate school and certified to advise M.A. and Ph.D. candidates and was in position to accept graduate advisees of my own. I quickly learned that if the graduate students were ambitious and career oriented they usually chose the older, more powerful professors as advisors; if they were insecure they chose the younger professors nearer to their own ages with whom they felt at ease. Most of the younger professors, for their part, visualized an entourage of advisees as evidence of success and some, to my astonishment for I had been unaware of any such practice at Wisconsin, actively recruited advisees with promises of publishing opportunities and jobs. Most of the older professors were scrupulous about avoiding any suggestion of the active recruitment of advisees and made no promises to graduate students of jobs and publishing opportunities.

Clifford Kirkpatrick in social psychology and the family and Lowry Nelson in rural sociology, among the older professors, gave most freely of ideas, time and energy to graduate advisees. Lowry Nelson had a large proportion of the foreign students in the department as advisees. I learned by accident that Lowry unostentatiously spent many hours correcting every line of their texts to make their English acceptable. However, the graduate students were, by and large, surprisingly realistic and the greater number who chose the older professors as advisors selected F. Stuart Chapin, who kept a strict account of every item of advice he gave. To ambitious students Chapin was the department's primary power symbol; Chapin, who had sponsored more Ph.D.s than any other professor in Minnesota sociology's history, in turn, visualized advisees as a prestige symbol. But Chapin was ambivalent about them and behaved toward them in a manner which suggested an attempt to control pillage by advisees. Whenever an advisee conferred with him, Chapin took out a note pad, placed a piece of carbon paper in it and at the conclusion of the conference wrote down a summary of all recommended suggestions He initialed this and gave the original to the advisee, keeping the carbon copy for his own files. Chapin was permitting no doubt as to where any suggestions he gave an advisee came from and was placing himself in position to prove it if necessary.[3]

Thus, shortly after joining the Minnesota sociology staff a number of experiences converged to dramatize to me the potential for pillage of students by their mentors or of teachers by their devoted followers. After coming back from military service I had heard at Wisconsin a number of stories of the exploitation of his advisees by Howard B. Becker; I had dismissed them as pure gossip. To be sure, Becker had written a one-sided contract, but still the joint enterprise promised to open publishing opportunities which, to me, far outweighed any consideration of material gain. However, suddenly after coming to Minnesota, the tricky suggestion had been made to break the contract and to tie me up for 20 years with an agreement not to publish in the area. The considerable work that I had done would unquestionably have gone into the project.[4] At the same time that this evidence of the extent to which I had been set up for possible exploitation was crashing on my consciousness, the success by some of the younger professors of recruiting advisees with promises of jobs and publishing opportunities, dramatized the interest of students in material and professional rewards from the advising process beyond the obtaining of degrees. The surprising behavior of Chapin (in making certain that he was in position to prove every scrap of advice he gave) indicated that even a scholar of national and international reputation was or thought he was potentially subject to exploitation.

In the midst of such accumulating evidence of the potential of the advising relationship for exploitation from either side, a graduate student made his appearance at Minnesota with a story that added new dimensions to the picture. For purpose of this narrative I shall call him Solomon Bachmann.

He had been teaching in a Caribbean university, though he had only a B.A. but had for a time held a position in the Bureau of Applied Social Research at Columbia. All his records indicated that he possessed superior mathematical skills. His story as to why he had left the bureau for a teaching job, but reapplied at Minnesota (where he was attracted by the school's reputation for empiricism) was as follows.

Solomon Bachmann had been appointed to the Bureau of Applied Social Research and for the better part of a year and a half had continued his studies and work without, apparently, being noticed by its directors. Then he was called in one day, handed a mass of data, and told: "See what you can make of this. Perhaps we can get an M. A. thesis out of it for you." He received no other instructions as to how to proceed or what to try to do with the material. He puzzled over the material for some months trying various operations on it, looking for some pattern. Eventually he hit upon an ingenious way of handling the material which caused it to fall into order. With some excitement he reported his findings to his sponsor.

His sponsor, was pleased, but said nothing about the M. A. A week later he heard that his sponsor had given a lecture on the findings, with no reference to him. A month later, a journal article appeared reporting the findings, but again with no reference to Solomon Bachmann. About six weeks after his work had been used without acknowledgement, Solomon Bachmann was again called in by his sponsor. To his astonishment he was again handed a box full of data and told: "Here, see what you can make of this. Perhaps we can get an M.A. thesis for you out of it."

When Sol Bachmann read the advertisement from a Caribbean university for an instructor to teach sociology, he applied for the job. When it came through he abandoned Columbia. However, after two years teaching, he realized that his career was going nowhere. He had applied for graduate work at the University of Minnesota not only because of its reputation as a department which appreciated quantitative methods, but because of Chapin's reputation for personal integrity.

When Chapin heard this story he pursued it far enough to ascertain to his own satisfaction that it was true. Chapin then proposed to the sociology faculty that Minnesota waive the requirement of the M.A. degree, admitting Solomon Bachmann directly into the Ph.D. program. This was done. Bachmann's superior performance in all quantitative areas confirmed the wisdom of Chapin's decision.

Since Solomon Bachmann's story of exploitation by members of an eastern research institution had come at the same time a number of other evidences of exploitation had been forced on my attention, I queried him about the matter at the time. "From the sound of things," I observed, "the way you were treated was more or less routine. Other students must also have been subject to exploitation. Why did they put up with it?"

To my surprise, Solomon Bachmann had long since accommodated himself to any bitterness he felt over his treatment at Columbia and answered quite objectively. "What other choice do the students have? A certain amount of exploitation is expected as part of appointment to the bureau. I made a mistake by getting sore and leaving, for I only hurt myself. If I had put up with it, once they had got out of me all they thought they legitimately could, I would have received the degree and they would have helped place me in a position."

The experience of Solomon Bachmann provided new perspective to the practice by some of the younger professors at Minnesota of actively recruiting graduate advisees.[5] How, I wondered, did a professor dare to promise publishing opportunities and jobs over which he had no control? Furthermore, if one actively recruited advisees, it would not be easy to discipline them if one felt it essential for the good of the department or for the long-range good of their careers. However, this reasoning was not shared and there was evidence that the same individuals who actively recruited advisees, took punitive action against them when they displayed too much independence or left to advise with someone else. Finally, there were repeated stories of how one of the individuals, who actively recruited advisees, carefully avoided giving help on any topic to an advisee until he had first published on it himself, but unhesitatingly incorporated into his own writing anything new that an advisee worked up on his own. Another of the young professors, who made extravagant promises in his active recruitment of advisees, eventually became enemies with them either because of alleged pillage or unfulfilled promises. This was related to me personally by one of the man's former advisees.

At the same time, the problem remained: in all fairness a student should be given credit for his own ideas and work, but his advisor should not be in position where he had to anticipate pillage if he gave his best thought and advice to the student's projects. A common sense solution to this problem was formulated by Roy G. Francis who joined the Minnesota Sociology Department during the 1950s. Francis maintained that it was his policy to joint publish as senior author any findings on a dissertation done under his direction in order that both he and the student receive credit for their respective work. I have never heard how consistently Francis followed this policy and, if so, how the students reacted to it. I did, however, hear that many students at Minnesota were furious at the suggestion that their advisors serve as senior author in the publication of their dissertation findings, no matter how much inspiration, work, and methodological assistance they received. The determination of *some* advisors to exploit their advisees was matched by the determination of *some* advisees to exploit their advisors.[6]

When I reflected on the practice of some of the younger professors of actively recruiting advisees in the light of Solomon Bachmann's experience at the bureau, I realized that my distaste for the practice stemmed from imposing inappropriate assumptions on it These same young professors who were recruiting advisees were modeling their professional objectives, including their advisee relationships, after the practice of such institutions as the bureau with its various contracts and grants for research. At the same time they were beginning to apply for research grants and to obtain time off from teaching to engage in research. They dreamed of building staffs of researchers paid out of funds under their control. Promises made to students before research money was available to sustain them, were incidental to assembling a research package. They did not visualize themselves as exploiting the students, for they intended to provide them with the opportunity for first-hand research experience by working side-by-side with them and had no doubt that they would be in position to recommend them for jobs as experienced researchers. It was essential to distinguish two different types of advising relationship: the professor-appointed and the student-elective.

While I had been in graduate school I had realized that the relation to their advisors by doctoral candidates in physics was usually quite different from those of us in the humanities and the social sciences. Some friends working for Ph.D.s in physics had been appointed by their advisors to work on projects their advisors had underway, using the equipment and materials the professor had under his control. At the time, those of us in the social sciences chose our own advisors and had to undertake dissertation projects we were able to fund ourselves. It was quite evident that such institutions as the Bureau of Applied Social Research represented behavioral science counterpart to on-going research projects in physics. A systematic transformation of the advisor-advisee relationship could be expected to accompany the new pattern imported from physics. From this point of view, the young professors in the post-war period who were both exploring prospects of funding research and inviting graduate students to become their advisees and research assistants, were the progressives.

In Berelson's study of *Graduate Education in the United States* he reported that more than one-third of all recent Ph.D.s agreed with the statement that "major professors often exploit doctoral candidates by keeping them as research assistant too long, by subordinating their interest to departmental or the professor's interest in research programs."[7] There was a discrepancy between Berelson's findings and those of the Bureau of Social Science Research in a survey published in 1963.[8] Laure Sharp opines that the differences between Berelson's findings and those of the Bureau of Social Science Research's survey may be explained by the fact that Berelson concentrated on the elite universities where research projects assume greater importance, while the Bureau of Social Science Research was reporting on the characteristics of a national cross-section which included many Ph.D. candidates from "lower-prestige graduate schools, where the pressures are of a different order. For the faculty in these institutions, awarding doctorates, rather than managing research projects, is perhaps still the area of greatest interest and professional accomplishment."[9]

Ann Heiss also took note of the fact that sometimes the advisor-advisee relationship is initiated not by the self choice of the student, but by appointment by the professor. This occurs more frequently in the hard sciences than in the humanities and behavioral sciences, though with the expansion of contract research it is also increasing in these areas. When it occurs it can be a highroad to opportunity and fame or a "kiss of death."[10]

Ann Heiss draws a distinction between the advisor and sponsor of the doctoral candidate which is found in some departments, however, in other graduate departments the sponsor and advisor are one and the same person. Where this distinction exists, the "advisor" has been converted into a formal or official position and the effective advisor is the sponsor.

However, the distinction between the two kinds of advising relationship associated with the voluntarily selected advisor, on the one hand, and the appointed advisee on the other is significant. Heiss took it for granted that the doctoral student ought to choose his own advisor, implying that the appointed advisee relationship is a deviation from the ideal. And, beyond quoting various student respondents who clearly belong to the class of appointed advisees, to the effect that this type of advising relationship could be either a tragedy or a triumph, she did not inquire further into the matter.

I have already reported my surprise on learning that some of the younger professors who joined the Minnesota department at the same time as I, were actively recruiting advisees. The older staff members shunned the practice, confirming the traditional conception of advising and clarifying the fact that some of the younger staff members were breaking from the tradition. The older staff members and I were still laboring under a pre-war depression psychology. These younger staff members were directing their professional energies toward the obtaining of research money in imitation of the practice in the powerful coastal universities. Actually, research money was becoming more available and the job market for Ph.D.'s was improving; the young liberals at the time did represent the wave of the future.

During the 1950s when I found myself wrestling for the first time with the implications of a changing style of doctoral relationship, I had before me not only the example of Solomon Bachmann's experience, but the unfolding story of C. Wright Mills's, relationship to my own Ph.D. advisor Hans Gerth. Mills had advised with Howard P. Becker, not with Gerth. However, Mills had instantly recognized that Gerth was more imaginative and learned. I do not think Mills took Gerth's classes for credit, but he audited all of them—some I believe more than once—and took careful notes. He also consulted with Gerth on all problems which interested him, for Gerth's stimulating suggestions for further study. Gerth, served more as an advisor to Mills than did Becker—possibly one source of the increasing tension between Mills and Becker.

Mills did not serve during World War II and when I returned to the Wisconsin campus after four years of military service, I discovered that Mills, who had been able to complete his Ph.D. and take a teaching position, had continued making excellent use of Gerth. During the war, Gerth had been giving courses to American military personnel in training for intellighnce work. As part of his course Gerth had translated many things from Max Weber which were useful in the interpretation of German thought and culture. Once Mills was out on his first teaching position he had collected Gerth's translations and approached Oxford Press with the proposal of a collection of Max Weber essays by himself and Gerth. Once Mills had obtained an expression of interest from Oxford, Mills approached Gerth, taking care not to mention the publisher, with the report: "I know where we can obtain a contract for a book of translations of Weber's essays, if my name is on it." Gerth agreed, specifying that he wished to write a brief intellectual biography of Weber to accompany the volume. A contract was signed. Gerth's translations of Weber were collected and gone over by Mills to smooth them for style. Gerth meanwhile went to work on his introductory essay. When the introduction was completed, although he had not contributed to the introduction, Mills insisted that his name also be on the introduction.[11] Largely on the basis of the publication of the volume, Mills was appointed at Columbia as an expert in German sociology.

Also during these years, Gerth had worked up a number of mimeographed essays which he was using in his course in social psychology at Wisconsin. Mills also collected these pieces and together with Gerth promoted a joint contract for a book to be written by himself and Gerth. In this case, Mills contributed somewhat more original work to the joint product though the manuscript primarily represented Gerth's work and Mills' rewrite. *Character and Social Structure* was the result.[12] Meanwhile, and as the 1950s wore on Mills's major books *White Collar* and *The Power Elite* appeared. Most of the basic ideas in them had come originally from Gerth's courses. I had taken these courses during the same time period as Mills and everywhere[13] I could detect the echoes of Gerth's lectures.

Whether or not one should describe Mills's relation to Gerth as the exploitation of a former teacher depends on how one wishes to interpret the term. Beyond any doubt, Gerth had contributed immeasurably more to *From Max Weber* than Mills who did not translate one sentence of the German or add a single footnote to the introductory essay. At the same time, Mills had the enterprise to obtain a contract for the collection which Gerth did not have to sign if he felt it was unfair. Although Gerth, again, added far more to *Character and Social Structure* than his junior co-author, it is not clear that he would ever have got out the volume without Mills's sustained drive. As for the many ideas taken over from Gerth's classes in *White Collar* and *The Power Elite*, Gerth, after all, had not taken the trouble to publish his own ideas, and Mills did submit his manuscripts to Gerth in advance of publication for his comments.

On one occasion I asked Gerth why he had put up with actions which most persons would define as rather brazen pillage. At that time Gerth pointed out to me among the many examples of Mills's unacknowledged appropriations he even copied some of Gerth's errors. Gerth was deeply ambivalent about Mills, simultaneously admiring his success, but repelled by his tactics. He confessed that on one occasion he had reproached Mills for the callousness in taking over the ideas of others only to receive the following brazen retort:

"Gerth, "when my family originally made their money in Texas it was by branding mavericks. Whenever they saw a cow running around without a brand on it, it was theirs. I figure that a loose idea floating around without a brand on it is fair game."

If one brought the experience by Solomon Bachmann in the Bureau of Applied Social Research into simultaneous perspective with Gerth's experience with C. Wright Mills, they could be seen as two styles of exploitation: of a graduate student by the director of his research and, of the teacher by a former student These were matters that were causing me concern when I first found myself under pressure to accept graduate student advisees of my own.

Toward an Advising Policy

When the first graduate students drifted into my office and indicated their desire to advise with me, I seriously wondered whether it might not be wise to decline. European, particularly German, scholars often cherished their advisors and remained friends with them for life. However, in Europe there had been some continuity in the forms of clientage appearing between Roman nobles and their dependents and between feudal lords and their vassals and the ties between professor and students in the universities. Such traditional forms of clientage had never taken root in the American universities and the relationship was not safeguarded by a traditional interpretation. Furthermore, even in Europe poisonous rivalries sometimes developed between former students and teachers.

At the same time, in graduate education and especially in its final phase, the Ph.D., the various aspects of the teaching, research and writing come into synthesis. Inevitably, the formalities that normally separate teachers and students are set aside. It is flattering to have young scholars who, for once, know what one is talking about, who hang appreciatively on one's words and who seek one's counsel. Down the road there may be disillusionment, double crossing and accusations of pillage, but for the moment every prospect is bright. Not to participate in graduate advising would be to fail to exploit one of the most crucial and exciting phases of the teaching profession. To undertake it without considering its hazards as well as its rewards was out of the question.

The fact that a new type of advising relationship was arising along side the traditional one, made it all the more imperative that one come to terms with the problem. The new advising relationship was an aspect of a shift in direction and emphasis from self-financed to institutionally financed (government or foundation or, even, university) research, from individual research to team research, from a system of reward that would place primary value on the research report rather than on the thoughtful interpretations of the theoretical monograph. There were some ironies in the trends. Wherever the funded research project made its appearance, the most prestigeful enterprise of the academic institution shifted to the production of research reports and publications and away from teaching, including graduate instruction. Graduate seminars often tended to be run as an adjunct to the research projects. The production of doctoral candidates was shifted to secondary importance and even, at times, viewed almost as distraction from the primary functions of the professors. There was suddenly more money available to finance graduate students, but they were no longer treated as individual scholars, and became the lowest paid workmen on research projects. Far from being systematically trained in all phases of research, they were often expected to subordinate their claims to the project, performing routine semi-clerical tasks.

Although all the signs pointed toward a structural change in graduate education, a radical reorientation around the funded research project, I found myself by temperament and background casting my lot with the traditional system. My speciality was a generality: theory and the history of thought. Few problems in theory and the history of thought invited team research and, in any case, while funds were increasingly being made available in almost every other area of the behavioral sciences, advances in theory and the history of thought appeared in the foreseeable future to depend on the traditional techniques of scholarship. I felt impelled to establish an advising policy for myself; it was a self conscious attempt to define the traditional doctoral advising pattern to make it serve my needs.

My own experience and the evidence around me of examples of the advising relationship, primarily offered negative injunctions rather than positive guidance. As far as I was concerned it had to be voluntary: freely chosen and freely terminable from either side. I had always been in the habit of choosing my own advisors and realized how awkward it would have been if someone had attempted to recruit me as his advisee if I had not wished to accept and faced negative sanctions because of failure to do so. The relationship had to be freely terminable by the advisor, for, it was inconceivable that an advisor retain an advisee with whom he could not work A relationship not terminable by the advisee was tyrannous. When I felt it necessary to complete my work in reasonable time at Wisconsin, it had required major special intervention by T. C. McCormick with the graduate school to obtain permission to change advisors. The events in connection with the contract for a joint introductory text with D. C. Heath, dramatized for me the potential exploitation I would have faced if I had not been able to terminate the relationship with Becker and complete my degree with Gerth. By the same token, it seemed to me, if an advisee left, it was inappropriate for an advisor to undertake punitive action against him because of it. Such abuse of power corrupted the entire teaching situation. By this time I had heard of situations where individuals could not work with their advisors, but were afraid to break away for fear of punitive action. In some instances, individuals dropped out of school or shifted to other universities and began their work over again because of entrapment with advisors they could neither work with or leave. The only rule I decided to follow with students who first freely chose to advice with me, but who later decided to leave—often after much work and thought and concern had been devoted to their problems and programs—was not to accept them back if they changed their minds. The principle was: the student who will leave an advisor once, will leave an advisor twice.[14]

A more difficult problem than deciding that the advisor-advisee relationship should be voluntary and freely terminable (without negative sanctions from the advisor[15]) from either side, was the degree of involvement or intimacy to be encouraged or tolerated. In the nature of the case graduate advising, particularly in the case of the Ph.D., tends to become informal and personal. Teacher and student quickly come to address one another by first names. Advisees may call their advisors at any hour of the day or night, and come over to their homes or apartments for emergency conferences. Advisor and advisee often remove a conference to the nearby tavern over a drink. They may party together and before long the advisee is coming and going informally as a member of the family. I have had advisees come to our home for hundreds of announced and unannounced visits enjoying coffee and cookies or turning up just before dinner to be invited to a meal.

One cannot work intimately with an individual who is facing, in the Ph.D., the most serious intellectual problems he has so far encountered in his life, without getting insight into his strengths and weaknesses. Furthermore, the situation often brings out into the open the advisee's personal problems and emotional difficulties. Moments of intimacy may encourage revealing confessionals. At the same time, the personal relation that develops between advisor and advisee, encourages candor on the part of the professor about his own problems, his colleagues, and departmental and university politics. An advisee may enjoy the intoxicating experience of getting the "inside picture" or the "low down"; the advisor the thrill of an admiring follower and confidant. It is quite easy for an advisor to drift into a degree of involvement with his advisee, from which he has difficulty extricating himself later. In the case of female advisors and female advisees, torrid love affairs may result with explosive consequences for the personal and professional lives of each.[16]

From the beginning it was clear to me that limitations had to be placed on the degree of intimacy permitted in the advisor-advisee relationship. I could understand F. Stuart Chapin's attempt to maintain the relationship, during the time I knew him, at a strictly formal level: meeting an advisee only on the basis of a formal appointment in his office, supplying him with an initialed note of all recommendations, and keeping a carbon copy for himself. Since I had recently spent four years in World War II, most of the time as an army officer and had seen the negative consequences when officers violated army regulations and fraternized with enlisted men, I could understand Chapin's purpose. However some students found Chapin's procedure intimidating and I personally could not see how I could work with a student on such a basis. At the same time, I was aware both from Wisconsin and Minnesota of the consequences of excessive intimacy between advisors and advisees. Viciously destructive conflicts sooner or later broke out between former intimates and, in the case of female advisees, at times love affairs led to divorce actions (where, for example, an advisor was already married but had to make an honest woman out of a pregnant advisee) and professional careers were side-tracked for a time.

However intimate an advisor and advisee became, it was essential that an ultimate wall of reserve divide them if an advisor was to perform his role effectively. In the end one had to be in position to discipline an advisee if he was out of line, to resist a line of argument that was inappropriate, and to terminate the relationship if it was no longer viable. These things could not be done if one were compromised in his relation to the advisee. How quickly role reversal could occur appeared when one advisee who was coming up with no ideas of his own, kept pressing me for suggestions as to possible thesis topics. This I did, outlining a suggestion in sufficient detail for him to check it out for himself. He returned in a day or two with the following comment:

"Professor Martindale," he said, "I do not want to be a whore and take the first thesis idea that is suggested to me. Will you give me some new ideas to consider?"

"I have a different suggestion," I replied. "Let us, for fun, reverse roles and I'll play the professor and you the student. You dream up some thesis topics. When you bring them to me I'll be happy to tell you what is wrong with them."

While I came to the conclusion that there was a line beyond which intimacy between advisor and advisee must not go, there was no rule that said where it should be. Students varied endlessly in shyness, aggression, trustworthiness, and discretion. A formula that worked with one individual was useless for another. In general I found it wise to quietly prevent a student from telling me his deepest personal secrets. I did not desire a kind of embarrassing information about him, which he would later hate me for knowing. At the same time, I thought it inappropriate for me to pour out my own problems and anxieties to students or to relate to them the more serious weaknesses of the staff. Students finish their work more easily and effectively when they are responding positively to the areas of strength of teachers they respect than when they are responding negatively to the problems and weaknesses of individuals they fear or despise. It is a disservice to students to fill them with fear and suspicion.

It seemed to me that not only should the advisor-advisee relation be kept voluntary and sufficient internal limitations be placed on the degree of intimacy to prevent role reversal, but some decision had to be made on the amount and kind of help to give advisees and what position to take toward publications that resulted. To refuse to give any advice to a student until one has first published on the matter and, at the same time, to treat as fair game for one's own publications anything new a student dreams up, might make sense in a long-range career strategy, but it spoils the advising process as an exciting activity for its own sake. If there is an intrinsic value in advising Ph.D. candidates, it lies in immersion in the problems and excitement of the first major research project of a young mind. To withhold assistance because of fear of theft and to study the results only with an idea as to what one can pillage from it, diminished the value of the experience. To insist on joint publications as senior author, while understandable, can be manipulative. No matter how much work an advisor puts into a thesis, the fact that the thesis is authored by the advisee alone defines its content as the advisee's property. However a student who expects unlimited help from an advisor, but does not intend to share credits with him is not learning how to be a colleague, but an entrepreneur.

The most rewarding approach to graduate student advising—was to view it as the privilege of a senior scholar in the socialization of the young. In this process, teaching, writing, and research all came, for once, into synthesis. The process had intrinsic values in its own right that were more important than any instrumental values for either advisor or advisee. I found it desirable to treat each individual advisee as if he were the only one I would ever have, for who knew whether I would ever have another. At the same time, this had to take place against the background realization that both of us were human, limited, and fallible. In the best case enduring friendships and loyalties would result from the relation, in the worst one could still look back on it with the realization that one had done the best one could.

In any case, it was the nature of the successful act of advising graduate students that one took status inferiors and transformed them into equals and friendly rivals. A healthy advisor-advisee relation had to undergo an internal evolution accommodating itself to the transformation. Once an advisee had successfully seen his candidate through the degree, he should no longer expect the same kind of deference he had once enjoyed as a teacher; nor should an ex-advisee expect from a former advisor the unreciprocated aid he had once taken for granted.

Notes

1. Robert K. Merton, "The Matthew Effect in Science," *Science* (1968), 156, 56-63.

2. An account of this incident appears in Don Martindale, *The Romance of a Profession* (St. Paul, Minn.: Windflower, 1976), pp. 89-90.

3. I first learned of this practice by Chapin from C. Dale Johnson, who was working on an M. A. with Chapin. I have no way of knowing how long during his advising career Chapin employed this device. It was my impression that it had been instituted as a safeguard after a major act of pillage by a graduate student. On one occasion when I asked him whether there was any problem of graduate advisees taking help and ideas without acknowledgement, he replied, "Students look eager and innocent, but they will not hesitate to steal your material without acknowledgement if you do not watch them carefully."

4. By sheer good fortune at the very time Becker was in the process of ousting me from his project to joint author an introductory text, E. D. Monachesi was invited me to join a project to produce one. Once the contract with Becker had been voided I offered my material to Monachesi. Within two months after my material had been made available, we were able to deliver a manuscript to Harper and Brothers. *The Elements of Sociology* appeared in 1951. Roger Krohn, who had started as a graduate student at Minnesota had spent some time in the Wisconsin sociology department during this period before returning to complete his work at Minnesota. He

reported that when the copy of *The Elements* came across Becker's desk he exclaimed, "My God, they stole the material." Of course, no part of Becker's material either directly or indirectly had been used in *The Elements*. Had we done so we would have undoubtedly been sued. Becker's reaction howevery left no doubt that, having had my material associated with his project for a while, had accustomed him to thinking of it as his own.

5. The most dictatorial way reported of recruiting graduate advisees at Minnesota was by the new chairman of one of the language departments. Upon taking over the headship, he simply transferred every graduate student in the department to himself Years later there were still evidences of the dismay this caused to staff and students alike.

6. In the late 1950s and the 1960s with increasing grants by foundations and various agencies of government for funded research, large numbers of graduate students were supported by such grants and obtained dissertation data in connection with them. Under these circumstances it became more frequent for publications to be senior authored by project directors. However, the advisors to dissertations completed outside such funded research often invested more time in them than did the project directors. Articles and monographs that resulted were infrequently joint authored.

7. Bernard Berelson, *Graduate Education in the United States* (New York: McGraw Hill, 1960), p. 152.

8. Bureau of Social Research. *Two Years After the College Degree: Work and Further Study Patterns*. National Science Foundation Report NSF 63-26 (Washington, D. C.: U. S. Government Printing Office, 1963).

9. Laure M. Sharp, *Education and Employment* (Baltimore: The Johns Hopkins Press, 1970), p. 27.

10. Ann M. Heiss, *Challenges to Graduate Schools* (San Francisco: Jossey-Bass, 1970), p. 151.

11. The product, of course, was *From Max Weber*, translated and edited by Hans Gerth and C. Wright Mills (New York: Oxford, 1946).

12. Hans Gerth and C. Wright Mills, *Character and Social Structure* (New York: Harcourt, Brace, 1953). I do not know all of the

complicated story behind the book. As I recall the initial contract was with D. C. Heath in the series which Howard P. Becker, Mills's advisor, was editor. However, by the time a manuscript was delivered Mills and Becker had fallen out and Becker was placing road blocks in the way of publication. Mills took matters into his hands, broke the contract and renegotiated a much more favorable one with Harcourt, Brace.

13. C. Wright Mills, *White Collar* (New York: Oxford, 1954) and *The Power Elite* (New York: Oxford, 1956).

14. The only exception I ever allowed to this rule was in the case of Dr. Myrtle Korenbaum. I was going on sabbatical and she asked to be permitted to shift advisors on the ground that she hoped to finish up the Ph.D. long before my return. I told her to go ahead. However, when I returned she had not even been able to get a dissertation started. When she asked, with some embarrassment, to be permitted to advise with me again, I made an exception in the rule because of the special circumstances of her request.

15. Although it seemed to me not only to be an abuse of power but to demean the professorial role to punish a former advisee who either had chosen to major with someone else or who had been asked to choose another advisor, this did not prevent some of them from spreading vicious lies and gossip about me—lies and gossip which some other faculty members eagerly consumed. If one retaliated in kind, it seemed to me, one reduced one's self to the same level. Since I knew how much work and effort I routively put into graduate student's projects, I rationalized the policy with the formula: "They've done enough damage to themselves already by depriving themselves of my help. If they can obtain an equivalent amount of aid from omeone else, more power to them." In any case, regardless of his or her provocation, I refused to pursue and punish a student once he had left me voluntarily or had been terminated.

16. On May 14, 1974 some of the female graduate students of the University of Minnesota appeared before the staff to protest sexual harassment by the staff. In the statement read by one young woman it was argued: "For the recipient, the problem of handling sexual innuendos, minor physical molestations and grosser forms of misconduct are compounded when the person initiating them has power

and influence over many aspects of the recipient's life. In such instances, the recipient may feel unable to use an explicit turn-down, brush-off or abusive response out of fear that such a response will jeopardize other valued outcomes, such as research help, recommendations, a good advising relationship, etc." Don Martindale, *The Romance of a Profession* (St. Paul, Minnesota: Windflower, 1976), p. 158.

CHAPTER III

ADVENTURES IN GRADUATE STUDENT ADVISING

One's image of the graduate student tends gradually to emerge out of varied experiences over time.

As an undergraduate in the 1930s at the University of Wisconsin, I was not initially aware that there was even a distinction between undergraduate and graduate students. However, at the time it was conventional to break large courses into lectures, which the entire class attended, and quiz sections. In the quiz sections the assistants of the professor took charge. One soon discovered the assistants to be a mixed lot: they were generally younger, better looking, and had not yet lost their hair or their shapes. Some supported the lecturer and undertook to clarify his presentations, some played an adversary role, often with unsubtle hints that they had the inside dope on the professor, some engaged in verbal pyrotechnics which transformed the course into a mystery, but quickly collapsed under questioning; some acted more like professors than the professors. These were the graduate students. The graduate student teaching assistants appeared between the undergraduate and the professor as his mouthpiece, intermediary, interpreter, and, at times, adversary.

I soon learned that the teaching assistants were quite capable of favoritism and soon discovered the practice among undergraduates in large classes with multiple quiz sections with different teaching assistants, of seeking to transfer out of the sections of teaching assistants with bad reputations. Where the professor himself taught one of the quiz sections, there was usually a mad scramble to get into it. It was the elite quiz section. By and large, the policies of the professor were more just, dependable, and more often tempered with mercy than were those of his TAs. I found myself trying to select courses as far as possible that had no graduate student TAs, for I never knew what kind of instructor I was getting until some potentially unfortunate experience occurred and at a time when it was no longer possible to change my program.

Two incidents involving brilliant scholars and teachers on the Wisconsin campus in the pre-war period shaped my first impressions of graduate students.

One, related by a close friend in English, who had taken a course from William Ellery Leonard, poet, philologist, and outstanding teacher. My friend had gone to Leonard's office after an examination to check on some questions he had and joined the line of other students waiting outside the office. While the undergraduates were queued up to be seen in sequence, a graduate student who was also taking the course came by. He simply brushed the waiting line of undergraduates aside, strode into Leonard's office, pointed to a prominent "D" on the cover of his blue book and demanded in an imperious voice.

"What's the meaning of this?"

The undergraduates who had been lined up, stepped aside in astonishment to watch the drama unfolding before their eyes.

Leonard responded to the demand by wheeling in his swivel chair, leaning toward his book shelf, grasping a volume of a two-volume collection of selections from English literature.

"Why, God damn you," Leonard said, as he swung back to hurl the volume with all his strength at the intruder.

The graduate student dodged out of the path of the missile, which hit the wall with such force that it shook the room, and beat a hasty retreat from Leonard's office. My friend stated that the particular graduate student disappeared from Leonard's class and he assumed either that he had voluntarily withdrawn or had been requested to leave.

The other incident occurred in a course on Medieval History which I took from George Clark Sellery, dean of the arts college and generally agreed to be one of the most able scholars and teachers on the campus. Sellery's lectures proved to be profoundly scholarly, inspired by an intense love of his material and always under the control of his common sense and wry humor. His quiz sections were remarkable. Neither before or after at the University of Wisconsin as an undergraduate I had ever experienced anything like them. Only later when I became a graduate student myself did I discover that Sellery ran his quiz sections in the manner graduate seminars were supposed to be run, but usually were not.

All students in the quiz section were required to read extensively among the most fundamental source materials of the period, with particular attention to works of classical or semi-classical status. Topics were assigned to individuals and each was required to give a report and be subject to examination by the professor and other students in the section. Undergraduate juniors and seniors (I was a junior at the time) found themselves in direct competition with graduate students, particularly graduate students in history.

One graduate student in history volunteered to give the lead-off report. With aplomb that was awe-inspiring to the undergraduates in the quiz section, he came to the meeting prepared to deliver his report armed only with a copy of the book. He had no paper and no notes, only a few slips of paper in the book here and there. When Dean Sellery turned the quiz section over to him, he responded with surpassing self-assurance. He placed the book before him. Took out his watch, and wound it ostentatiously, placing it beside his book. He cleared his throat and prepared to begin.

As this was going on a deep silence fell over the seminar that had the quiet of the lull before a hurricane. I found myself stealing a furtive glance at the Dean. I noted that the other undergraduates had their faces averted as if they were afraid to look. A deep stillness had fallen around the Dean; his countenance was a face of stone.

Within moments the self-assurance of the graduate student began to fade. He read a passage or two and then repeated in his own words what he had read in language less interesting than the original. The recital began to trail off, the words began to stick in his throat, and he abruptly broke off his report. For the first time I stole a look at my watch—the report had lasted exactly six minutes.

With the report over before the period was seriously under way, the silence deepened. No one dared to speak and to the last individual we awaited Sellery's response. For his part, Sellery allowed a full thirty seconds—a thirty seconds that seemed like an eternity—to pass without moving or saying a word. If his purpose was to permit the full gravity of the situation to sink in, he succeeded. Then, he casually leaned over, and picked up the book on which the report was to have been delivered.

"This," Sellery said, "is one of the richest documents of the Middle Ages. *Even* [he stressed the word] if one examines it casually, its richness is clear."

He flipped through a few pages. "Now, listen to this." He read a passage of surprising illumination and made a few casual comments on it. He flipped further. "Or this," he said, and again read a passage. "Those," Sellery observed, "who draw a sharp distinction between the Middle Ages and modern times could contemplate such observations as these with profit." Again he read a revealing passage.

"I would recommend, Mr. Wyman," Sellery said as he closed the book and for the first time looked directly at the graduate student, "that you take this book back, and *read* it [he stressed the word "read"] and *be prepared* to report on it next week." The quiz section was dismissed.

It was after this incident that one of the undergraduate members of the quiz section got up nerve to ask the Dean.

"Dean Sellery, how long should our papers be?"

A small smile flickered at the corners of the Dean's mouth, as if he relished the question and had been patiently awaiting it.

"That question," he said, "always reminds me of a story told about Abraham Lincoln. He was asked, 'How long should a man's legs be?' Abe said, 'Long enough to reach the ground.'"

After this helpful bit of advice I got busy on my own paper for the quiz section. Among other things I read through 17 of the 22 volumes of Thomas Aquinas's *Summa Theologica*. And, for the first time in my life, I wrote a thirty page paper.

These two incidents dramatized for me, as an undergraduate, the high opinion graduate students often had of themselves, the fact that they frequently acted more like professors than professors, but, also, that in the minds of the professors—at least in the minds of the better professors—they were still students.

In the 1930s I developed my first impressions of the graduate student as an undergraduate. I earned the B.A. in

1939. The 1940s proved to be the period of my own graduate work: prior to the war as a graduate student first in philosophy, then in sociology; after the war when I finished my own degree, part of the time as both instructor and graduate student.

In the early 1940s, prior to America's entry into World War II, the country was still stagnated in economic depression. I quickly discovered that the graduate students divided into two types: the younger full-time graduate students and a few old timers who were working part-time outside and who had working wives. The old timers were mines of lore about graduate work and the professors. They had an ambivalent relation to the departments, for it was policy of the departments to force graduate students out on their own as soon as possible, to prevent their transforming temporary low-paid positions intended for the support of new graduate students into a way of life. However, the old timers were reluctant to permit their ties to the university to be cut, for all responsibility for placing graduates into positions was abandoned as soon as they could be forced out of the nest.

The younger graduate students (most were unmarried, for these were still times when one member of a family was dropped as soon as the other obtained work) were inclined to reduce outside work and restrict their style of life to a minimum placing all effort into the completion of the degree. However, as the actual completion of the degree became imminent, there was often a dramatic change of pace. Work on the degree was often stopped altogether while the individual tried to obtain a position. If he was unable to do so he sometimes took outside work part-time or married, but kept his ties with the university —his life style was recycled into that of an old timer.

The source of the hubris of the graduate student was clear. Graduate students had reduced course loads, they presented papers that were graded on quality and presentation, the familiar anxiety over the repeated crises of course examinations was largely over. Much more of their time was spent on projects which, if not completely under substantive control, were at least under individual time control—the writing of papers, the passing of language examinations, the preparation for preliminary examinations and last, and most important of all, the research and writing on a dissertation were largely at the individual's discretion. A graduate student had many opportunities to act as an autonomous scholar.

There were additional occasions for graduate student hubris. They worked closely with professors; flaws not visible at a distance became glaring. In the course of researching a subject unexpected limitations in a professor's knowledge often leaped into view. In conducting laboratories or quiz sections quiz instructors were rarely challenged, by the undergraduates, and tempted into infatuation with the sound of their own voices.

I was drafted before I could complete my preliminary written examinations and the dissertation I had underway had to be scrapped. After some four years in the Army of the United States, as an enlisted man and an officer both stateside and overseas, I returned to resume graduate work once again. I completed my written examinations, took a job and ended up teaching in my own department while I completed the dissertation.

A number of things meanwhile had changed the character of graduate study from its pre-war character. Members of my generation whose graduate careers had been interrupted by war were inclined to resume a depression psychylogy when we returned to the scenes of our old crimes. However, a bustling new cohort of individuals was undertaking graduate work with a different outlook. Their educations had been delayed by the war, but so had the opportunity to live as they chose. They were receiving G. I. support for their educations and did not have to scramble for teaching and research assistantships. Their world outlook had also been transformed by the fact that the war ended the depression and America had emerged as the foremost world power. A war-torn world looked in considerable measure to the American economic machine for restoration. The colleges were expanding. Professors were in demand. The new generation of graduate students tended to marry, to live in apartments rather than in rooming houses; they purchased cars as soon as they became available. Their inclination was not to monastically reduce life to bare necessities shifting their energies to speeding up graduate progress, but, as far as possible, develop a full middle-class life style without major deprivations even while they were still graduate students. No longer was it true that if one party to a marriage obtained a job, the other lost his or hers. Hence, between a husband's G. I. benefits or his teaching assistantship and the wife's job, a couple in which one or both members was in graduate school, could maintain approximately the same standard of life as graduate students as they expected to enjoy upon completion of their degrees.

Also, the graduate students had changed their images of themselves from that of their pre-war counterparts and having, in the immediate post-war period, had experience in the army and having sources of support and economic prospects not available in the pre-war period, were more inclined to organize and seek collective control over their fates. At the University of Wisconsin, Madison, in the immediate post-war years, they organized, protested, and transformed the statistics requirements which had been a major source of anxiety before the war. However the distinction between "old timers" and "eager beavers" did not disappear.

Writing in 1970 Laure Sharp still distinguished two types of graduate students: student with clear goals, working on stipends and studying full time; drifters and hangers on with uncertain goals, pursuing their studies part time.[1] In my experience in philosophy and sociology at Wisconsin as graduate student and instructor and at Minnesota as a professor, the distinction between the younger full-time professional student and the somewhat older part-time student (setting aside women who either left school to marry after the B. A. or who started graduate school, married and dropped out as full-time students, reducing their work to part-time until their children were sufficiently grown to return to graduate work full-time) was, if anything, clearer and qualitatively differents in the pre-war than in the post-war period. The old timers before the war were trying to keep their professional careers alive. The hangers-on after the war had been trapped by life styles inconsistent with academic work.

When I joined the Minnesota staff in 1948 F. Stuart Chapin was still its chairman and very much in charge of its policies toward graduate students. He had not changed his pre-war attitude, that continued pressure had to be kept on graduate students to prevent them from settling down in graduate student positions and occupying them indefinitely. Chapin's reasoning, often expressed in staff meetings, was that if pressure was not placed to get the students off the available support positions, there simply were not enough students to keep the graduate program viable. Chapin did not notice that the graduate students in the post-war period clung to their positions for altogether different reasons than those in the pre-war period. In the pre-war period many students actually delayed, when they could, completing the degree until they were able to obtain teaching or research positions, whereafter they completed them as fast as possible. In the post-war period, by contrast, the entire image of their position by many graduate students had suffered a sea of change; many more were inclined to place first priority on maintaining an adequate standard of life, and to shift completion of the degree to second priority. Many graduates, thus, started out in the first category of student distinguished by Sharp, but ended up in the second. Only this will account for the length of time, which has disturbed so many students of graduate education, it had taken the average graduate student to complete his work. In Sibley's words:

> If John Fiske's theory is valid, that prolongation of infancy is characteristic of the higher stages of evolution, Ph.D.'s in sociology must represent a very high order of beings, for in terms of the average time elapsing between bachelor's and doctor's degrees they are tied with historians for first place on the list of social scientists, with a median interval of 9.9 years...The median age at receipt of the doctor's degree in sociology has recently been about 32 1/2 years; it was slightly higher for the generations whose studies were interrupted by World War II, but is now close to the pre-war level.[2]

Berelson had estimated that only half of the time between degrees was devoted to full-time graduate study.[3]

In the set of studies initiated through its Manpower Studies Group in 1959 by the National Science Foundation and continued for ten years, a large cross section of the June 1958 graduating class, including recipients of bachelor's, master's and professional degrees, was chosen for study.[4] In 1963 these same graduates were contacted for a second, more detailed follow-up study. Sharp reports: "For the great majority of Ph.D.'s graduate study is a slow process. After receiving the master's degree in 1958, only ten percent of the men and three percent of the women pursuing Ph.D.s had received them five years later."[5]

In the period immediately following World War II at Minnesota graduate students in sociology conformed to this pattern. They were taking anywhere from five to ten years after the B. A., to complete the Ph.D. At the time a Plan A., M. A. was considered essential for the evaluation of a graduate student's potential for undertaking the Ph.D. This entailed the completion of 27 credits work (18 credits in the major and 9 in a minor field), the passing of one language requirement and the writing of a research thesis (normally a 75- to 80-page report on a research project). The individual also had to pass an M. A. written examination, a four-hour general examination. Theoretically one could complete the M. A. in a year, practically it was usually stretched over two to four years. A task faced by the M. A. examining committee (consisting of the chairman of the committee, a second professor from the major and a professor from the minor field) was to evaluate the performance of the student to that point and make a recommendation as to his potential for undertaking the Ph.D.

The Ph.D. consisted of three year's course work (which included the M. A. work), the completion of two languages (or one language and a tool subject), the taking and passing of the comprehensive written examinations and the passing of a preliminary oral examination. Only successful completion of the oral constituted admission to candidacy for the Ph.D. The Ph.D. dissertation required on the average of one full-time year's work (between choosing a topic, completing background reading, gathering data, analyzing them and writing up the results).

Theoretically, one could complete everything other than the dissertation in about three years (the M.A., the languages, the preliminary examinations); practically the M.A. was usually stretched out over three to four years. A good part of the time five to six years had gone by before the preliminary examinations were completed. By this time there was growing restiveness to get out on a job. But when a job was taken, the average doctoral candidate found it expedient to set aside the dissertation and spend full time keeping up with the work, learning the ropes and the like. However, as I had learned long before when the dissertation I had started was interrupted by military service, a long delay is usually disastrous to a dissertation. When a doctoral candidate takes a job and tries to fight his way through the dissertation despite all the distractions almost anything can happen.

I came to the Minnesota campus in the Fall quarter of 1948 meeting the first new graduate students who had not yet chosen advisors in that year. Also from 1948 on there would be students coming into graduate school who had my upper division classes as undergraduates. The senior professors in the department included F. Stuart Chapin, Lowry Nelson, Clifford Kirkpatrick and Elio D. Monachesi. Among the assistant professors were Douglas Marshall, Arnold Rose, Theodore Caplow and Neal Gross. Although some students began to major with me from the beginning and although I put a few candidates through the M. A. in the early 1950s, I did not put my first Ph.D. candidate through the final oral for the Ph.D. until 1955. It was not until the end of the 1950s that the number of Ph.D. candidates majoring with me began to accumulate (See appendix).

When the first graduate students drifted into my office and (despite the fact that I was a complete unknown and did not have the prestige and power of the older professors of the Minnesota department and was systematically shunning all temptations to actively recruit advisees) asked to major with me. I accepted this as an unavoidable condition of the teaching profession of a major university. When I was first asked what they should do for their M. A. and Ph.D. theses, I was transported back to the days in the early 1940s, some ten years before, when I had made an appointment with Howard P. Becker to ask a similar question. I still recalled the acute bafflement at his self-assured assertion: "I want you to do a dissertation on the stranger," an assertion unaccompanied by any statement of which of the endlessly conceivable types of stranger he wished studied (outside a few remaining small communities in which all individuals were born, lived and died in the same circle of acquaintances, the experience of being a stranger—that is coming as a relative unknown into a new circle of situation or circumstance— was universal, moreover even in the small closed community the newborn was often described as "the little stranger").

Becker did not, at the time, tell me that he had recently read Simmel's essay on "The Stranger" which, was available only in German at the time. Had he done so I would have got out the German edition and translated the essay for myself. I did not discover this on my own, for at the time I was too preoccupied with other requirements to be able to systematically peruse the sociological literature in German. When at a later date I encountered the essay, I realized that had I known about it, I could have explored the possibility with Becker of formulating various of Simmel's generalizations as hypotheses for empirical test.

When I had pressed Becker for specific direction, he indicated that he had done his own Ph.D. dissertation under Robert E. Park at the University of Chicago on the metic, the resident aliens of the Ancient Greek city states. I did some research on the metics myself and discovered that they were free men but not full citizens of the city states. They were typically individuals from other cities who did not have citizenship in the city state where they resided and, as a result, were excluded from the political and military affairs of the community. At the same time much of the business enterprise of the ancient city-state was in the hands of metics and frequently entailed legal and political problems which forced them to enter into a client relationship with full citizens in order to have representation before the courts. Such arrangements provided the metics with political and legal protection and were profitable to the full citizens.

While I explored the role of the metic in Antiquity for the first time and learned interesting things about it, my confusion as to what the metic had to do with a dissertation on "the stranger" was increased. It was evident that the majority of metics in Ancient Athens, for example, were not strangers at all, but had been born in the city state and had lived there all their lives. I was too naive at the time to realize that Howard Becker was probably trying to suggest either (1) I continue his study of the metic with the hope of turning it into something publishable (I did know that Becker was desperately anxious to publish his study of the metic but had so far failed[6]) or (2) was resorting to an expedient common to many scholars when they first undertake their own advising, putting his advisee to the task of replicating his Ph.D. dissertation as the only type of dissertation he knows how to complete.

Whichever possibility Becker had in mind, I had no way of knowing and Becker did not offer to lend me his own Ph.D. dissertation for review. Copies were not available in the Wisconsin library and I was not aware, at the time, that one could request the dissertation from the University of Chicago on interlibrary loan. Moreover, I was too busy with my other work to devote full time to the problems of a dissertation and leaped to the conclusion that just as Becker had studied one type of "stranger" (in an unusually extended meaning of that term) in the metic, he probably wished me to study another.

In all of this, Becker and other members of the department at the time provided no methodological guidance on thesis writing. I found myself returning to my philosophy courses in logic and scientific method and particularly consulting the philosophers on these problems. I found John Dewey's logic to be particularly helpful. It seemed to me that in his *Logic* Dewey provided a clearer statement of the requirements of a dissertation in social science than I was able to obtain from any of the Wisconsin professors of sociology in the 1940s.

In and of itself, the existential world is such that an unlimited variety of selective discriminations is possible. A problem decides the selection which is actually instituted in any given case. In what is called *common sense*, the problem is that of some use-enjoyment. In science, the generic problem is promotion of controlled inquiry. Since the required control can be obtained only through the intermediation of abstract interrelated conceptions, inductive existential determinations are conducted with constant reference to institution and application of conceptions deductively interrelated with one another, while the conceptions are chosen and ordered with reference to ultimate existential application.[7]

This formulation seemed to define the task of a Ph.D. dissertation in social science as the advancement of knowledge of social life. Dewey was unquestionably correct in his assertion that actual experience could be interpreted in endlessly varied ways; only when one had a problem did one's study become specific. Dewey had compactly summarized the difference between common sense and scientific problems: common sense problems were a matter of pragmatic day-to-day importance, or in Dewey's terms matters of "some use-enjoyment"; scientific problems were a matter of the development of theory or of explanation. In short, in science one advanced a theory to explain a conceptual problem and one gathered the facts in the light of the theory to prove or disprove it.

Dewey had even devoted a chapter of his *Logic* to "Social Inquiry" which specifically laid down principles for social science study. Among these principles were the following:

> All inquiry proceeds within a cultural matrix which is ultimately determined by the nature of social relations.[8]

> A genuine problem is one set by existential problematic *situations*. In social inquiry, genuine problems are set only by actual social situations which are themselves conflicting and confused.[9]

> Inquiry into social phenomena involves judgments of evaluation, for they can be understood only in terms of eventuations to which they are capable of moving.[10]

> Fact-finding procedures are necessary for (1) determination of *problems* and for (2) provision of data that indicate and test *hypotheses;* while formulation of conceptual structures and frames of reference is necessary to guide observation in discriminating and ordering data. The immature state of social inquiry may thus be measured by the extent to which these two operations of fact-finding and of setting up theoretical ends are carried on independently of each other, with the consequence that factual propositions on one side and conceptual or theoretical structures on the other are regarded each as final and complete in itself by one or another school.[11]

These propositions spelled out the problem of social science research in specific detail. During my forced absence from the campus during service in World War II, after abandoning the topic of the stranger I relied on these injunctions to rough out a problem and gather data for a thesis, looking forward to the time when I would eventually be able to return and complete my degree work.

By the time I was faced with the question from advisees of my own "what should I do for a dissertation?" I had made my own choice among current conceptualizations. The Ph.D. dissertation was variously conceived as an exemplary performance revealing a candidate's fitness to perform original research, as a contribution to knowledge, a monograph, a treatise on a particular subject, a theoretical argument intended to advance the understanding of social events. The conception of the dissertation as a monograph incorporated the other ideas in itself. My answers to this question were always: What problem do you wish to study. How do you propose to solve it?

I was well aware, by this time, that the conception of the dissertation as a monograph was no guarantee that work done in its name would be significant. No one could serve in a major university without hearing stories of the specialist in some area of history or literature or economics who forced his Ph.D's to work for years on trivial problems or minutiae of his field. His counterpart in the social sciences, was the professor with a pet project of his own, who blessed his advisee and research assistant with the privilege of working out some minor problem on his project, on which he was lucky to be able to publish a research note. The tendency that William James had described as the "Ph.D. Octopus" was still very much part of the graduate scene.[12]

In view of the perennial character of the complaint that professors put students to work on petty and insignificant problems, a surprisingly high proportion of the graduate students studied by Heiss reported favorable attitudes toward the help received from their advisors in selection of the research projects (62%), framing their research designs (76%), and writing their dissertations (82%).[13]

From the beginning I found it necessary to resist current myths and practices among graduate students which if permitted unchecked would transform their dissertations into mechanical exercises or demonstrations of empty virtuosity.

One practice that had to be resisted was the tendency by graduate students to review the dissertations completed in the department, picking one to copy as a sort of cookbook recipe on the same or a related problem. Closely related to this was the tendency to take some methodological device and look for substantive material to fit into it. The trouble with the cookbook recipe approach and the methodologically pre-committed approach to a Ph.D. dissertation was that they minimized the learning possible from an original involvement with data and turned thesis work into clever carpentry. Methodological precommitments and cookbook recipes were Procrustean beds, inclining a student to do violence to the facts to make them fit. Whatever else was true, method had to serve problem and theory rather than forcing problem and theory into the advance suppositions of a particular method or dissertation formula.

The single most important myth that had to be resisted was the cynical notion that "The smart way to handle a dissertation is to take something simple and trivial and get it done as fast as possible." Even rudimentary observation would have shown the individuals who repeated this myth that it was false. Almost every dissertation which was begun with the conviction that it was a superficial and trivial was, never finished. Dissertations started under this supposition which blew up were an embarrassment to their sponsors who were not anxious to herald their discomfort. A moment's reflection would have shown why the myth was false. By convention a Ph.D. dissertation represented a quantity of achievement that required approximately one full year's work. Anyone who choose the Ph.D. as the occasion for a trivial dissertation was bestowing a year—which should have been the most original and creative of his entire life—on a project which was, by his own definition, insignificant. The effect was to cheapen what otherwise could be a year of fulfillment in qualification for the profession. Whenever problems arose in the dissertation, begun under such assumptions—and there is no such thing as a dissertation that does not face some problems, sometime—the energy and enthusiasm was lacking to solve them: why should one extend serious effort on problems which by one's own definition are trivial to begin with. The "trivial dissertation" had a way of never getting done at all though it often dragged out for several years. Eventually after much lost time, the candidate who seriously wanted the degree chose a topic he was interested in and started over.

My advice to all advisees in the teeth of this remarkably persistent graduate student myth was emphatic: "Do not choose a dissertation topic unless it is so important to you that you would be willing to do it even if you were not required to do a dissertation. If the topic is important to him, an individual will always find the imagination and energy to solve its problems no matter how serious they appear at first. If a topic is unimportant to him, an individual will find it impossible to complete it, for when the problems arise, and they unavoidably will, he will not have the energy and imagination to solve them."

An offshoot of the myth of the quickie dissertation was the fear by many graduate students of first-hand field research. German research scholars had long talked about the "stubbornness" of the facts. Dewey had this in mind when he spoke of the "unlimited variety of selective discriminations" possible whenever one confronted the "existential world." No student who went forth with an open mind to deal with the world of fact has ever managed to avoid renewed appreciation of the discrepancies between tentative conceptualizations and the great amorphous world of fact. No research establishment is without its loud noises of pain, as researchers struggle to win a new level of understanding of the world. The sounds of agony coming from those Ph.D. students who are in the field actually seeking to deal with the existential world, fill the novice who has not adentured outside the ivory tower with terror. This is a major reason for the persistent myth that the way to succeed is the "quickie" dissertation. Some students will go to almost any length to avoid first-hand data gathering, to find some body of data that has already been gathered to subject to secondary analysis.

I have found it almost useless to explain that the saving of time in working with secondary data was usually more apparent than real. Though important studies at times emerge from the secondary analysis of data gathered for another purpose, such data rarely fits some new design with any precision. Almost invariably the things one most needs for a decisive proof or disproof are lacking. Significant publications rarely emerged from the analysis of data gathered for different purposes than those originally intended. Although, over the years, some students insisted on doing dissertations on secondary data, no such dissertation done under my direction was ever published although numerous dissertations done on original data under my direction have been published in monographic form.

In general my own experience conforms rather closely to that of the majority of the faculty as reported in Ann

Heiss's 1970 study. "On the whole, graduate faculty respondents were more satisfied with the dissertation requirement than they were with any other Ph.D. requirement; 88 percent expressed approval of it as presently required, 9 percent thought that it should be modified, and less than one percent thought it should be dropped."[14]

There is some truth to the idea that has been around since the early decades of the twentieth century, that some professors are inclined to put their doctoral candidates to work on trivial problems, but, in my experience, before a dissertation was eventually agreed upon in nine out of ten cases, I have found it desirable to expand the theoretical focus of the design of the doctoral candidate rather than to narrow it. To be sure, a problem often went through two general stages: (1) in the first stage the doctoral candidate came up with a topic that was so loose and broad that it was best characterized as an area of general interest rather than a problem; (2) when the candidate was pressed toward a specific issue and when the need for evidence and proof were insisted upon, the candidate was inclined to reduce his problem to such small and immediately manageable size that it began to lose theoretical relevance. The conceptions of the Ph.D. as a routine exercise and the tendency to view the doctoral thesis as a self-serving professional ideology had both to be overcome. Most candidates did not want to contribute to knowledge; they wanted to complete the degree and get out on the job. Most said, if one asked them the meaning of the Ph.D., that it was a professional union card. The dissertation was the last and to some the most frustrating obstacle of all.

It required some time for me to come to terms with the realization that my own and most of graduate faculty's conception of the doctorate did not closely correspond to the conception held by many doctoral candidates. By the time they are ready to undertake the dissertation, the ordinary graduate student is socialized into the profession and pays lip service to the ideal, that the doctoral dissertation should be a contribution to knowledge. However, by this time he has been some years in the process of completing course work, writing off language requirements, and passing his preliminary examinations. Meanwhile, in the post-war period, the typical graduate student had married and was trying to maintain a middle-class style of life on a limited budget. He was far more anxious to get out into the field as a "real" professor than to recycle his thinking and plunge into the doctoral dissertation in the exhilarating knowledge that at least he is free to plunge into pure research as an autonomous scholar. Ideally, the Ph.D. might be a privilege to do original work; practically it is the last and biggest hurdle.

The most difficult problem I found myself facing as an advisor was persuading degree candidates to remain in school and complete the degree before accepting a position. In Sharp's study it was found that a large proportion of the Ph.D. candidates were quite satisfied with their progress. Sixty-four percent of the men and 60 percent of the women of 1959 recipients of master's degrees were satisfied with their rate of progress toward the Ph.D.[15] Many candidates in my experience insisted on taking teaching positions before completion of the dissertation, even though they were quite able to remain in school longer without changing their standard of living. Sharp observed: "One feels that while it would be good to get through school faster, it is not really too uncomfortable to combine some work, part-time study, and a family life. In fact, in terms of life style, this may be preferable to the prolonged, aided graduate student status that seldom provides a truly comfortable way of living."[16]

However, it is unnecessary to rationalize the graduate students' casualness about completing their degrees in the immediate post-war period: it was a part of the graduate student culture. Sometimes when a student short-circuited the process and earned the degree before looking for a job, it was by accident.

A young woman who was working toward the degree dropped by my office one day with her husband who was also enrolled in a degree program. She was making rather slow progress on her dissertation because she was working as a teaching assistant and was finding it necessary to type all of her husband's draft (he was unable to type) and correct his style (she had majored in English literature as an undergraduate) as well as make up for deficiencies in her undergraduate sociology background. Her parents had visited the young couple and had come to the conclusion that she was trying to do too much.

Her father who was a small business man had written to suggest that in view of the number of things she was trying to do at once (including all the mechanical and editorial work on her husband's dissertation as well as her own) she allow him to finance her year of study, give up her assistantship and spend full time on degree work. When I asked whether she was prepared to accept this offer she exclaimed: "Of course not, I'm married and independent. I no longer need his support."

"Why don't you look at it this way." I suggested. "Your father knows you can support yourself. But he's worried that you are doing too much. He wants to see you complete the degree, not ruin your health. Why don't you accept his offer and finish the degree faster and then pay him back, by helping put your sisters through school ?"

She left with her husband, quite unconvinced. A week later she stopped by my office, alone. Her eyes were flashing.

"I'm married to a *schlemiel*," she said. "Would you believe it, my husband wrote to my father and told him that he accepted his offer of support in lieu of a TA-ship for himself. My father never made the offer to him. He intends to let me keep my assistantship, clean up his English, do all his typing, and try to work on my own dissertation, while he has nothing to do but work on the thesis."

She instantly resigned her own assistantship and her father ended up supporting both young people. However, the incident had a happy result, for both completed their dissertations and passed their final orals before accepting positions and leaving the campus. They might easily have had to take jobs and spend an additional five years at the task.

While this experience illustrates the efficiency with which the degree could be finished when circumstances made completion a priority, another experience may illustrate the risks when the candidate leaves the campus for teaching or research.

In one instance an advisee received a fellowship from a newly established institute and was on field placement on a handsome stipend that supported him and his wife to complete a community study. Nothing was apparently happening for a year and a half of the two-year grant, and the director of the institute was deeply worried, for the whole funding of his institute depended on his showing effective results soon. A number of projects the institute had supported had blown up; he simply could not have any additional failures I asked that both husband and wife be sent back to confer with me over his progress on his research and dissertation. When I conferred with them he was in a disturbed, almost catatonic state. Hence, I stressed to both of them the importance of keeping in touch and urged her to keep the correspondence and help keep the project moving, indicating that as things came in I would critique them and outline what further had to be done step-by-step.

Once she took over the correspondence after they returned to the field there were regular weekly progress reports. Suggestions were followed and corrections were made regularly and routinely. When it came to the final most crucial phase of the dissertation I wrote an unusually long and detailed letter explaining precisely what steps had to be taken. There was a long silence and then I received a startling letter from her.

"Would you, please," she asked, "explain in detail what *I* should do next. I have never written a dissertation before, and I don't have the slightest idea as to the next step." I made a copy of my original letter and sent it on, but received an even more astonishing letter. "Please disregard my request," she said. "John is telling me how to finish the dissertation. His suggestions are brilliant."

There was only one possible interpretation of these events. The advisee's wife had been doing more than acting as secretary. She had been writing the entire dissertation. Despite the fact that she had only completed two years of undergraduate work in the university, she had been following instructions and completing the entire dissertation alone. The strange business over the mail could only have meant that her husband had intercepted and opened mail addressed to her, had pocketed it and was transmitting on to her advice that I had given as coming from himself. I never learned whether she ever discovered what happened for after he received the degree her husband divorced her and married a woman he felt was more worthy to be the wife of a Ph.D. in sociology from the University of Minnesita.

Some time later, I heard from a mutual friend that the same individual was talking to a young scholar who had taken a job in the same sociology department before completing his dissertation. The newcomer was complaining about the difficulty of finding time to work on his thesis. He was advised: "The way to get a dissertation completed is to get a wife who knows how to write." This was said humorously as a grand joke.

Incidentally, the completion of this particular dissertation proved to be important in obtaining the permanent funding for the research institute that financed it. The dissertation done under these circumstances became the model for the first dozen or so studies completed under the institute's auspices.

In another instance a candidate left for a research position in the last stages of his degree program. He was sidetracked and did not finally complete the doctorate until 20 years later. When his professional career would how been terminated without it.

Taking a position, whether in teaching or research, was a potential disaster to dissertation plans, quite apart from the intelligence or personality of the candidate. In the typical case, the first thing that happened to a candidate upon obtaining a job is that all interest was drained away from his dissertation. Psychologically his energies were regrouped around a whole new set of concerns and he often had to prepare himself both intellectually and emotionally for his new role. This was the only way to account for the fact that once he had accepted a job, the candidate usually did not finish his dissertation before taking it even when he had plenty of time to do so.

Once on the job a candidate, even with the best of intentions, rarely found time during the first year to do significant work on his dissertation. This, despite the fact that he may have made firm resolutions to devote at least a little systematic time to it. However, the intervals between periods when he actually tried to work on the thesis were so filled with matters remote from it, that he often wasted more time recovering the context and getting in the mood to work on the dissertation than he did accomplishing work on it. In the majority of cases during the first year on the job no work was done on the dissertation.

Another simple psychological principle came into play when an individual tried to pick up a dissertation after a year's absence from it. When one rationalizes one's failure to work on a project through an entire year, one develops a cycle of excuses good for one year. It is as if the project had been sealed behind a wall of force. It is only a fraction as difficult to rationalize failure to work on the project the following year. Once one has gone through an entire year without touching a project, ten years is as one.

If one had put a good deal of work into a dissertation before accepting a job, there is deep frustration in the thought of giving up the project and seeing all one's work go down the drain. Meanwhile, there may well be considerable developments in the field of the dissertation which had to be restudied before one is in the same position as originally. By the time this happens, the candidate is trapped between contradictory tendencies: resistance to dropping a topic; resistance to moving ahead on it; frustration over work that must be redone. The psychological forces centering on the dissertation form a kind of emotional vortex which drains away more and more time and effort without producing positive results.

Quite often the individual who has become trapped by these contradictory forces is able to free himself from them only when he is threatened by the loss of his position if he does not complete the degree. After advising a number of candidates in these situations I came to the conclusion that once a candidate has become so entrapped, he is usually wiser to drop the topic and choose another on which he can at least make a fresh start. It has often required the combined effect of outside pressure and a new topic to move a candidate off dead center where he can neither drop nor make progress with a given dissertation.

I soon came to the conclusion that it was irresponsible advising, not to encourage a candidate to complete the dissertation before accepting a position. I also began systematically to press advisees toward a decision on an ultimate Ph.D. dissertation as early in their graduate programs as possible. Inasmuch as, until 1970, the sociology department at Minnesota had treated completion of a Plan A M. A. (that is a master's degree with a research thesis) to be a prerequisite to admission to the doctoral program, I tried, whenever possible, to persuade advisees to undertake the M. A. in the same area in which they ultimately hoped to complete the Ph.D.

Where this strategy was successful, so much momentum had been generated in the candidate to complete the dissertation that many did so before taking positions in the field. Moreover, the effect of carrying out field research first on a M.A. and later on the Ph.D. resulted in a fair number of dissertations which were good enough for monographic publication.

Meanwhile, my decision to treat graduate advising as an activity with intrinsic values from which I had as much to learn as the student himself, meant that I was to advise dissertations over much of the range of sociology and its methods from laboratory experiments, through statistical studies, to field studies, and from participant observation studies to studies in the sociology of knowledge based on content analysis. I found that it was necessary in the first few studies of a given type to work almost as hard on the topic as the student himself. Substantively, I advised studies in social organization, social change, social stratification, the sociology of knowledge, science, medicine, and art as well as the sociology of community and the sociology of ethnicity. Although it was time-consuming and often required as much or more preparation than I had to put on my courses, graduate advising permitted me to explore, along with students, many different sorts of theoretical and methodological problems first hand. And although I always encouraged students to publish their work exclusively for themselves either in monographic or article form and often worked to put their materials into shape for such purpose, I was enriched by the experience. I declined to compete with them, but published my ideas in my own books and essays apart from their dissertations.

There were many happy and amusing adventures along the way. One involved a husband and wife team who were working on dissertations at the same time. I talked them into doing companion studies of a local ethnic group at a time second generation community studies were common, but third generation studies were rare. My own observation suggested that major transformations were occurring in the third generation, on the one hand, and in the stratification system of the ethnic community, on the other. Hence I proposed that one of them study the generational changes of the given ethnic community and the other the stratification structure, and when everything was completed to put both studies together into a community portrait that ought to be eminently publishable.

When the husband brought his wife for a conference, he sat to one side, presumably occupied with other things, while I advised her on her next step. He always insisted on coming alone to his own conferences. Thus, he always heard what advice I gave to her; she did not hear what advice I gave to him. However, after a conference with her the next time I received a section of his dissertation everything I had advised his wife was incorporated into his text. I cut out such material a number of times and warned him against continuing the practice. However, when it continued I finally said in some exasperation to them both.

"Please, this practice of putting identical material in both dissertations has got to stop. I will, of course, cut it out, but if this persists I shall have to refuse to advise you further. I beg you to look at how this will appear to an outside scholar if you persist in putting identical material into each dissertation. It is bad enough to have a husband and wife doing simultaneous dissertations with the same advisor on the same ethnic community without having identical material appearing in each. Can you imagine how I will look if I permit this? What would I say to anyone who asks: 'What is Martindale doing as a dissertation advisor? Is he running garment makers specials; two for the price of one?' I do not want you even to read each other's dissertation until the final orals are passed. Then you can put the two dissertations together into what I am sure will be a single publishable monograph."

When the pair obtained their degress and came to the house to say goodbye for the last time and started away, she returned sundenly, as if because of an after-thought. "By the way," she said in tones of heavy sarcasm. "Is it all right if we start sleeping together again?"

They departed on a gust of laughter.

Notes

1. Laure M. Sharp, *Education and Employment: The Early Careers of College Graduates* (Baltimore: The Johns Hopkins Press, 1970), p. 13. See also National Science Foundation, *Graduate Student Support and Manpower Resources in Graduate Science Education* (Fall, 1965; Fall, 1966) (Washington, D. C.: U. S. Goverment Printing Office, 1968).

2. Elbridge Sibley, *The Education of Sociologists in the United States* (New York: Russell Sage Foundation. 1963), pp. 99–100.

3. Bernard Berelson, *Graduate Education in the United States* (New York: McGraw-Hill, 1960), p. 160.

4. Bureau of Social Science Research, *Two Years After the College Degree: Work and Further Study Patterns.* National Science Foundation Report, NSF 63–26 (Washington), D. C.: U. S. Government Printing Office, 1963).

5. Sharp. *Education and Employment*, p. 25.

6. I had become acutely aware, at this time, of the fact that Howard P. Becker and Robert Redfield had both earned the Ph.D. under Park at approximately the same time. Both men were preoccupied with the distinction between sacred and secular communities, concepts which represented Park's translation of Toennies's concepts *Gemeinschaft and Gesellschaft*. Becker seemed to be acutely sensitive to the fact that Redfield had outdistanced him in the competition, not only because he had married Park's daughter, becoming the son-in-law of the master, but because he had published his own dissertation on *The Folk Culture of Yucatan* while Becker had failed to publish his dissertation on *The Metic*.

7. John Dewey, *Logic: The Theory of Inquiry* (New York: Henry Holt, 1938), p. 484,

8. Ibid., p. 487.

9. Ibid., p. 498.

10. Ibid., p. 502.

11. Ibid., p. 507.

12. William James, "The Ph.D. Octopus," in *Memories and Studies* (New York: Longmans, Green, 1911), pp. 329-347. See also, H. J. Laski, "American Education," Chapter 8 in *The American Democracy, A Commentary and Interpretation* (New York: Viking, 1948).

13. Ann M. Heiss, *Challenges to Graduate Schools* (San Francisco: Jossey-Bass, 1970), p. 128.

14. Ibid., p. 129-130.

15. Sharp. *Education and Employment*, p. 134.

16. Ibid., p. 28.

CHAPTER IV

TRANSFERS, DROPOUTS, AND FAILURES

It has been found that nearly half of the persons entering the Ph.D. program drop out at some stage.[1] Speaking for sociology, Sibley observed.

> Surprisingly few data are available on rates of elimination and withdrawal from graduate study in various institutions, though it is well known that a majority of students leave for one reason or another before attaining the doctoral degree. Formal and informal procedures for shifting out unqualified students not only differ from place to place but frequently change from year to year in the same department. Nearly everywhere a considerable exodus takes place at the end of the first year and another on receipt of the M.A. degree. Once a student has surmounted the M.A. hurdle and has been permitted to continue work for the Ph.D. degree, expulsion for failure in final examinations is quite rare.[2]

At the time Sibley wrote this (1963) it was still true at the University of Minnesota sociology department that a Plan A, M.A. which involved a research thesis (in contrast to a Plan B, M.A. which had special papers, more course work and was treated as a terminal M.A.) was still visualized as the primary screening device for determining whether students were qualified for admission to the Ph D. program At the time, in the early 1960s, most of the major schools still followed this practice, however even then some of them had dropped the M.A. altogether as a prerequisite for admission to their doctoral programs. Graduate students were admitted directly into Ph.D. work. The M.A. was in such cases occasionally given, but as a sort of consolation prize for doctoral dropouts. For example, a former editor of

Houghton Mifflin told me that after spending ten years in sociology at Harvard, it eventually became clear that he was never going to complete the degree. Thereupon some members of the faculty urged him at least to take the M.A. He reported that he had protested: "How can I when it is a booby prize." He was told, "The rest of the country doesn't know that."

During the 1960s there was an increasing tendency to drop the M.A. altogether as a prerequisite for entering the Ph.D. program. In 1970 Minnesota followed suit, although the M.A. is still offered if the student wishes to take it along the way. With the elimination of the M.A. as a prerequisite for the Ph.D. the number of M.A.s has rapidly declined and almost all of those taken are Plan B type, once conceived as a terminal degree. I have been unable to locate any studies which seek to determine whether the elimination of the M.A. as a requirement for the Ph.D. has made any difference in either the speed with which the Ph.D. is completed (reasons could be advanced for its cutting the time at least in half) or in the attrition rate.

In Ann Heiss's study it was found that 8 percent of the public university respondents and 6 percent of those in private institutions in the sample transferred to another field after they began Ph.D. studies giving as reasons disappointment with their programs, inducements by professors in the new field (or offers of better scholarships or financial subsidies), and personality conflicts with their advisors. More than one-third of the respondents reported that they had interrupted their studies or had been tempted to drop out of their doctoral program for a variety of reasons: 25 percent reported lack of interest in the field; 26 percent reported lack of interest by the faculty in students; 14 percent reported poor relationships with their advisors; 40 percent reported boredom with their studies; 44 percent reported disillusionment with graduate education.[3]

The high attrition rate for doctoral candidates which, according to Tucker, may run as high as 50 percent, would be a source of concern even if those who drop out of doctoral programs or who are forced out were the weakest because of the amount of time that is lost from what ought to be the most productive and creative period in a young person's life.[4] However, there is wide consensus—ranging from graduate students, through faculty members, to departmental chairmen and deans—that often creative students who may or may not fit a departmental image are lost.[5]

The problem of attrition from doctoral programs could be visualized as a crucial test of the adequacy of the advisor-advisee relationship, particularly when it entails the loss of many of the most intelligent and creative of the candidates. The single most intimate relationship into which the graduate student enters in graduate work is with his advisor (or possibly his sponsor when distinguished from his dissertation advisor as is the case in some graduate departments). The advisor or advisor-sponsor acts or, at least, can act as the general pilot to the student around the shoals of graduate study through all its phases to the completion of the final oral.

In my own case, I was keenly aware of the origin of my own view of the graduate advisor relationship in my own experiences. By the time I had transferred to sociology the whimsicalities of professors and the accidents of circumstance had made a thorough impression on me. I had decided that ultimately the graduate student was on his own and the wisest procedure was to find the shortest path through the jungles of graduate study. The principle was: if one waited long enough for something to happen, it would and 99 times out of a 100 the change would be disagreeable.

Rational planning of one's program, for example, depends on a stable situation in the immediately foreseeable future—say three to four years. However, the requirements for the Ph.D. rarely remain unchanged for long. There is a slow change of requirements from year to year so that at the end of a five-year period the differences are so marked they would hardly have been recognizable to someone who had been away that long. Moreover, as professors move through their career phases and eventually retire, the alternation of generations makes itself felt on the doctoral program. In most departments this reaches a climax at seven to ten year intervals. A new generation takes over and insists upon relatively complete revision of the graduate program to make it conform to its requirements. Graduate students seeking to complete their programs during a period of generational revolution often face arbitrary changes of requirements and psychological milieus of relatively complete anarchy. Doctoral advising takes place against a changing background of the processes in the graduate faculty in which the advisor himself is an actor.

However, even this does not exhaust the processes which complicate the relation between advisor and advisee, for as has already been noted doctoral study has emerged as a way of life for graduates with processes and laws of its own. The typical college graduate is 22 years of age before he is in a position to contemplate graduate school. Since the development of the child labor laws, on the one hand, and increasing technological transformation of the economy on the other—the one tending to keep the young person by law off the permanent labor market, the other reducing the need of the economy for unskilled labor—the student will rarely have had other than incidental job experience. He has been a student all his life and is disinclined to welcome graduate school in which for another ten years he may remain in such pre-adult status. Graduate student status has emerged as a period in which the individual marries (or sets up a companionate marriage), rents his own apartment, owns a car, enjoys his own personal property (radios, Hi-Fi, color television), takes summer vacations (to the mountains, seashore, backpacking in the wilderness) like any other member of the middle class. The graduate student may intend to practice family planning, but pregnancies will happen and he or she must decide whether to obtain an abortion or start their family with the accompanying new financial obligations. I have known graduate student couples who, faced with the break up of their marriages, decided to have a child. The principle seemed to be before things can become better, they must be made worse.

In the 1950s with so many graduate students receiving G. I. veteran's benefits, on the one hand, and with the persistence of the patriarchal pattern which tended to keep the wife at home or on the job while her husband completed his degree work, the maintenance of a decent middle-class style of life by graduate males was often quite compatible with regular progress toward the degree. However, with the rise of the women's liberation movement and pressure for increasing numbers of women to stay in graduate school along with their husbands, maintenance of what both viewed as an adequate style of life became more difficult.

Throughout the period of the 1960s and 70s the changing norms were also accompanied by a rising divorce rate among graduate students. Among the kinds of situations that can be disastrous to progress toward the doctorate and which may frustrate the best direction an advisor can give are illustrated by: the graduate student who was making good progress until his wife left him to marry one of his professors; the wife who has been working hard to keep the family together until she discovers her husband has been two-timing her with other graduate women and sues for divorce; the arrangement that was working beautifully until an unwanted child arrived creating major financial crises; the married husband-wife team which was doing fairly well with the man deferring his progress to promote her career only to find himself divorced when she ended up with the doctorate before him.

The manner in which the battle of the sexes may frustrate degree plans is indicated in the quotation from a graduate student by Heiss to the effect that one young woman in his acquaintance stopped with the M.A. in order not to exceed her husband's level of education. In a close parallel to this I had one young woman as an advisee whose husband was working in another department. I had placed her on a heavy schedule (with the hope that she would be able to complete the degree requirements at the same time as her husband), lined up her requirements for optimum orderly completion and put her to work on an M.A. She performed brilliantly. A few days after her completion of the M.A. she dropped by my office to tell me that, while she intended to continue course work, she was abandoning plans for the doctorate.

"But you are doing brilliantly," I said. "Why stop now?"

"That's the problem," was her astonishing answer. "My husband's work has not been going well. My progress has been driving him crazy."

"Did he say he wanted you to stop?"

"No. But I get the message. If he comes home and I am studying, he slams the door, stomps across the floor, and turns on the Hi-Fi loud enough to enrage the neighbors so they pound on the wall. If I keep on I'm afraid it will wreck my marriage."

"Of course, it is your life and you have to run it in the manner that best suits you," I counseled. "However, you both should realize that at any time in graduate work these things can turn around. A year from now you may find yourself bogged down, while everything is going smoothly for him. There has to be some give and take. My best advice would be to shift your work to low key so you are not so much of a threat, but plan and take your courses and other requirements in a manner to move your work toward the doctorate. Otherwise, some day both of you may find yourselves hating one another because you had the opportunity to complete the doctorate, but did not."

She followed this advice. He never did get his work properly underway, gave up a fellowship and delivered an ultimatum: "You can do what you damned please, stay here and complete your work or come with me." Rather than permit her marriage to collapse she left with him. However, she had completed enough of the requirements to be able to finish the rest of her work later and write off her remaining requirements and her dissertation in absentia returning only for her examinations. His position improved and he is immensely proud of his wife today.

The advisor-advisee relationship, thus, is not only complicated in its own right, but is in part trapped between the social processes of the graduate faculty and the emergence of the period of graduate study for the students as a quasi-permanent way of life. Very often tensions from one or other of these two processes are at the bottom of the so-called personality antagonisms between student and teacher. The advising relationship must be visualized not only in terms of its successes, but also in terms of its partial and complete failures.

Not all persons who originally choose a graduate advisor remain with him. Some leave him voluntarily; some are

Transfer Advisees and Others : 1948–1979

Type	Number	Ultimate Destiny
Voluntary Transfers	8	2 dropped out of the degree program 3 completed their degrees 2 are still in process, one after 19 years 1 returned to complete degree with her original advisor
Rejected or advised to choose other advisors	7	4 dropped out of the degree program 2 completed sociology degrees 1 transferred to another department where he completed the Ph.D.
Advisees who failed to complete degree work	10	2 dropped out of the degree program 6 failed to get through preliminary examinations 1 developed a fatal illness 1 failed to complete dissertation
Advisees in process as of October 1977	5	

requested to leave. And not all persons an advisor accepts and who remain with him manage to complete the degree. Table 1 summarizes to the best of my recollection my experience with these various categories of advisees.

Of those persons who voluntarily chose other advisors: some were recruited by other staff members by promises of professional aid in getting jobs and obtaining publications. At least two became antagonistic toward me because they felt that I was pressing them too hard to get on with their degree work. One advisee left because I was going on sabbatical and she thought that by transferring to another advisor she could complete her degree work long before I returned. Although some professors were offended by an advisee's departure, I could not see the problem in that light. I worked too hard and spent too much time on advisees to wish for a moment to press unwanted aid on an unreceptive student. A student who did not wish to be speeded on his course had the right to select his own rate of progress. One of those who left because he felt that I was being unfairly urgent eventually finished the Ph.D. after 12 years in process; another is still in process after 19 years. I could sympathize with the student who transferred to another advisor while I was on sabbatical—after all, long ago I had transferred from Becker to Gerth because Becker was on leave and I was finding it impossible to get on with the dissertation. However, when I returned from sabbatical and the student had not even got started with her new advisor, she requested permission to return which I granted.

Three persons were rejected as advisees: two because of personality antagonisms that made further work with them difficult if not impossible; one person was rejected because of my conviction that he was at the limit of his ability. I did not want to further waste his time and have this on my conscience. Four other persons left voluntarily when I advised them to consider transferring to other advisors because of aggression directed by other members of the graduate staff toward my advisees. Not all persons who were urged, at the time, to seriously consider changing advisors chose to do so. Some felt that they had more to lose by transferring than by staying and remained to take their chances with me.

However, over the period from 1948 to 1977 covered by this review, ten advisees who remained with me failed to complete the Ph.D. Two of my Ph.D. candidates dropped out of the degree program without even attempting the written preliminary examinations. Six took the examinations but failed to get through them; two persons who completed the written and oral preliminary examinations nevertheless failed to complete the Ph.D.—one developed a fatal illness, the other simply stopped all work on the dissertation for unexplained reasons.

It required some time for me to come to terms with the realization that the failure of an advisee to obtain the degree was not always a tragedy. Some intelligent and personable individuals continued on through the university, into graduate school and a degree program simply out of inertia. They are competent enough to stay afloat, but not motivated by genuine interest in the Ph.D. They continue to drift until such time that the going gets rough and they either fail and are forced to try other things or they drift off into the by ways. There was a function performed by tough preliminary examinations, both written and oral, quite apart from the attempt to establish qualifications for the final step in the degree process, the admission to candidacy. Preliminary examinations, when they are tough, test the resolve of the candidate and the seriousness of his intentions.

Both personality and circumstance play a role in long delays in the completion of degrees or in drop-outs from degree programs. Degree candidates have all the emotional hang-ups as the rest of the population; these tend to be exacerbated by the high tension of a degree program. Moreover, when a husband or wife of a candidate is unhappy with his or her lot, the degree program of the partner is often sabotaged. The husband or wife, as the case may be, leaves or starts divorce action at the very time when support is most needed, as, for example, when the student is about to take major examinations. The loss of emotional support at crucial times is sometimes temporarily, sometimes permanently, disastrous. The candidate for the highest academic degree has enough problems without having simultaneously to undertake the battle of the sexes.

The manner in which personality traits which are usually positive in intellectual contexts can cooperate with institutional arrangements that are usually desirable to bring about negative effects is illustrated by the case of Balwant Nevaskar. Balwant came from an old Brahmin family of Poona, India, a family that had owned a Hindu temple since the Indian Middle Ages. He belonged to a branch of the family that had been Christian for some generations. Balwant had earned the B.A. from the University of Bombay. He had come to the University of Minnesota to study philosophy, but became interested in sociology and earned the M.A.

He had a gentle personality, a cheerful disposition, and an intense interest in intellectual matters. I have known few individuals more sensitive to the needs of others. However, he was also the kind of person who does his best work when he is not under pressure. Under pressure he usually put his worst foot forward and produced work of lower quality than was routine for him when not under stress. There are always some much types around a university who have rich productive careers, for they do not require crises to do their best work.

At the time Balwant was ready to present himself for the preliminary written examinations in sociology, the two other students who took the examinations at the same time, were neither as well informed or as intelligent. Ironically, because of the tension of the examination, they passed, Balwant failed. At the time the department had a rule which permitted any student failing his written as a whole to routinely come up for a second try. Balwant studied intensively although it was not further study that he needed. When he came up for a second trial his tension was worse than on the first try. He could not even physically sit still and on retake performed more poorly than on the first examination. The department did not grant permission for a third try.

Balwant had married a North Dakota girl and was working as a table waiter at the time of his disaster on the examinations. Since I was convinced that his problems were emotional rather than intellectual, I urged him to take a teaching job for a time to restore his confidence and then apply to some new university. He obtained a position teaching sociology at Gustavus Adolphus College at St. Peter, Minnesota. He did an outstanding job teaching, and his classes were quickly filled to overflowing. His wife enrolled in the college to work for a teaching certificate about which she had always dreamed. Balwant soon won the respect of his professional colleagues and the administration for his good humor and integrity.

When Balwant was returning by plane to India because of illness in the family, he met Dr. Irawati Karve of Deccan College of the University of Poona. He told her the story of his problems with the prelims at Minnesota and about his teaching since. She urged him to enroll in the graduate program of the University of Poona. Also Dr. Karve approved of his dissertation, comparing the religious ethic of the Quakers of the United States and the Jains of India, which Balwant had started under my direction during his graduate work at Minnesota.

Balwant not only completed the Ph.D. at the University of Poona with the thesis originally begun while a student at Minnesota, but returned to teach at Augsburg College of Minneapolis and later at the University of Puget Sound at Tacoma, Washington where, for a time, he became chairperson. Balwant's thesis was accepted as a monograph by Greenwood Press and published under the title, *Capitalists Without Capitalism: the Jains of India and the Quakers of the West.*

A second advisee who took the preliminary written examinations and who failed them, as a whole, twice and was eliminated under the rules had a language problem. He had been a police lieutenant in Seoul, Korea who lost his position in a change of administrations and had come to the United States to retool and wait until it was strategic to return to Korea in another capacity. He had earned M.A. degrees in police administration and sociology at another midwestern university. However, his spoken and written English were deficient and, particularly under the tension of the examination, resulted in a rather incoherent text. It is quite possible that had he been permitted, as I proposed at the time, to write his examinations in Korean and have them translated into English they would have been adequate to satisfy the examiners, for he was highly intelligent.

He had a wife and three children to support and transferring to another school to complete the degree presented serious economic problems. Since he had failed to obtain the Ph.D. he could not return to Korea without a serious loss of face. After teaching a year and half at the Memorial University of Newfoundland during which his statistic courses were attended by the faculty as well as all graduate students in sociology, he obtained a position as research analyst for the Minnesota Department of Corrections, became an American citizen, bought a house, began to put his children through school, and wrote numerous articles for publication which again proved beyond doubt his basic intellectual competence.

Two other persons who had proceeded as far as the written preliminary examinations failed the examinations as a whole on first try: one seems simply to have drifted by inertia to the point where he was technically ready for the written preliminary examinations, but he had not studied seriously for them. He never exercised the option of trying the examinations again after failure on first try. The other student who dropped out after a first failure on the writtens was from Ethiopia and, though highly intelligent, was much harrassed by events in his homeland where some of his family and his friends had been executed. Though his passport had been revoked, he feared to return home, lest he be executed himself. Many persons acquainted with him had been impressed by his imagination, his sensitivity and his intelligence. His poor performance on the writtens was unquestionably related to his situation. After the examination he dropped from sight without ever presenting himself for a second try.

Two advisees who failed to get through the preliminary written examinations remain to be accounted for. However their stories have been told in detail in *The Romance of a Profession;* it is unnecessary to retell them here.[6]

Notes

1. A. Tucker, *Factors Related to Attrition Among Doctoral Students.* Cooperative Research Project N. 1146, U. S. Office of Education, Michigan State University, 1964.

2. Elbridge Sibley, *The Education of Sociologists in the United States* (New York: Russell Sage Foundation, 1963), p. 96.

3. Ann Heiss, *Challenges to Graduate Schools* (San Francisco: Jossey-Bass, 1970), pp. 178-179.

4. C. R. Rogers, *Graduate Education in Psychology: A Passionate Statement* (La Jolla, California: Western Institute of Behavioral Science, 1964).

5. Heiss, *Challenges to Graduate Schools*, p. 179.

6. Don Martindale, *The Romance of a Profession* (Saint Paul, Minn.: Windflower Publishing Co., 1976).

CHAPTER V

EX-ADVISEES AS COLLEAGUES

I started advising graduate students with the realization that the Ph.D. dissertation was a rite of passage. It was the highest point in a student's career—and the last. The ambivalence that accompanied it were characteristics of situations in which one is torn in two directions at once: backward toward protected student status, forward toward independent professorial status. Characteristically such periods—like falling in love—are, at once, so temporary in fact, but psychologically so seeming permanent. Advisees at such times often say with heartfelt intensity: "You will always be my teacher." They mean it profoundly—for the moment.

Former advisors and advisees who later come to blows and engage in bitter vendettas, are attempting to retain pre-degree relations into post-degree circumstances. Some advisors are incapable of accepting former advisees as full colleagues; some advisees try to maintain a life-long relation of whining dependency on a former advisor or seek to pillage him as ruthlessly as they once pillaged their parents.

Once a student has obtained his degree, his advisor is no longer in position to speed or slow his academic progress. However, the student is in varying degrees still dependent on his advisor and other teachers: they have information about job opportunities, they must be counted upon for good recommendations, they may have access to publications and are usually more knowledgeable as to how to go about publishing. Furthermore, few persons remain long in their first jobs, hence, after a year or two ex-advisees may appeal to their former advisors for new job leads and recommendations. Meanwhile, advisors who hear of openings or are asked for special recommendations are in position to alert former students to opportunities to improve their professional standing. Still further down the road when ex-advisees become eligible for tenure and promotion their old advisors may again be asked for recommendations. There is normally a kind of transition period in which the ex-advisee is gradually evolving into a state of full professional equality with his former teachers.

In the case of advisees who already have jobs at the time they complete their Ph.D.'s, jobs which they do not intend to change, this period of successively diminishing dependence is lacking. In most such instances I observed that with the degree a wall of silence almost immediately descends between advisor and advisee, although in a few cases evidence later came to light that at least some individuals remained friendly in a distant fashion. But in many cases there was not sufficient interest in the old advisor to correspond with him or even answer Christmas greetings. I did not attribute this to antagonism, but to indifference and the evident meaning completion of the Ph D. had for such individuals. Such persons were not visualizing the Ph.D. as a positive stage in their professional careers, for they already had positions with which they were satisfied. Rather, completing the Ph.D. in such cases was a negative or defensive activity resulting from the fact that they would lose their positions if the degree were not completed. Hence their silence and indifference toward their Ph.D. advisors did not necessarily represent ingratitude or dislike: their advisors were simply part of a negative and disagreeable activity which they were relieved to have behind them and which they were anxious to forget as rapidly as possible.

In the case of an advisee who had a job, but who was anxious to get out of the hole he felt himself in and obtain a better one or who did not have a position at all, the completion of the Ph.D. normally had positive rather than negative meaning. Such an advisee looked beyond the degree itself to something more from his advisor: to jobs, to recommendations and to publications. Once the degree was completed relations with the advisor recycled along a new level of dependencies and expectations, which, however, moved both parties closer to status equality. Genuine friendship—and not its various counterfeits such as tricky manipulativeness or psychopathic flattery which turns instantly into poisonous denunciation when an ever-expanding series of demands for favors from the advisor is not met—could, in this transition period, develop between senior and junior colleagues.

Sooner or later these advisees, too, obtain jobs which they intend to keep and they may manage to publish and begin to establish professional identities of their own. It is an unavoidable consequence of the teacher-student relation that the umbilical cord that holds a student to his teacher is cut. This is the critical time in which it becomes clear whether advisor and advisee have evolved into fully independent colleagues, between whom permanent ties of friendship and affection persist. I consider myself fortunate, for with some of my former-advisees I remain close friends.

It was not long after my own advisees began to strike out on their own that I began to hear that some of them were repeating my lectures word for word and giving my advice to students as their own. This was not surprising, for long ago when Louis Wirth had been invited to the Minnesota campus during summer session I had urged my advisees not to miss his classes. He was reputed to be the best urban sociologist and theorist in the United States. One of my advisees, C. Dale Johnson, returned from Wirth's classes with the report that he had already heard Wirth's lectures down to end including his very jokes from Wirth's former student and Ph.D. advisee, Arnold Rose. Sociologists, it seems, are often quite serious when they speak about standing on the shoulders of giants.

At the time this dramatic bit of information was received about one of my colleagues at Minnesota, it placed the teaching profession in new light. While still at Wisconsin and before I had finished my own degree, some of the graduate students who had completed their preliminary examinations had been auditing my lectures and taking copious notes. When I asked them what on earth they were doing since they had completed all degree requirements other than their dissertations, I received the sanguine reply: "We have to go out and teach next year; we're building up a good set of lecture notes." I had dismissed this at the time as humor.

However, I recalled this incident when the information came that Rose had been repeating Louis Wirth's lectures—and, who knows, what others of his former University of Chicago professors. This explained to me, in part, not only why Rose had the reputation as a brilliant lecturer, but also why he was able to spend such an enormous amount of time on his writing. From the moment he arrived as a young scholar in the Minnesota department, an astonishing volume of writing was produced. At the same time, although we were close to the same age, I found my lectures and teaching were consuming the greater bulk of my time.

Since there was never the slightest doubt about Rose's ability, the practice of repackaging the lectures of his teachers could not be put down to incompetence. That he was saving time and placing his efforts where they were professionally most significant, on research and writing, was evident. Moreover, as he published, Rose was beginning to revise his lectures in terms of his writing. Hence, over time, his lectures were gradually being overhauled and made into his own image. Rose, however, pursued a quiet policy of never lecturing on an idea until he had published it first. Rose took to heart C. Wright Mills's principle: an unbranded idea is a Maverick.

I realized, in reflecting on Rose's practice, that he could not be an isolated case in his use of the lectures of former professors. The graduate students who had been auditing my lectures for their own, had not been joking. The repackaging of the lectures of teachers has probably been going on as long as the university has existed. Besides the written traditions of the universities, which are like froth welling up on a rushing torrent, is the great current of its oral traditions, sometimes stagnating in sloughs, at other times rushing in cataracts.

Also in reflecting on this tendency by students to work out of the lectures of their own teachers, I realized that it was a practice which must appear in variations from the repetition of a teacher's lectures almost by rote, to the employment of his formulations as a starting point for further elaboration. Moreover, the point also was brought emphatically home to me that both temperament and circumstance had conspired to make this short-cut to professional success inaccessible to me.

I had gone to college during the depression in part as an escape from a poor economic situation. I was self-supporting, and inclined to respond to university life as an intrinsic rather than an instrumental value. My own pattern of inferiority feelings forced me always toward testing myself by the university's requirements: I had to do my own study, write my own papers and, later, work up my own lectures. I envied Rose's capacity to simply transmit on the oral traditions of his teachers, while he concentrated on the professionally invaluable activities of research and publishing, but I was incapable of proceeding in this way.

Meanwhile, I had moved into sociology with an M.A. in philosophy and had never taken the introductory courses. The first time I took introductory sociology was when I taught it myself. When, after a single semester on the circuit, I was called into residence at the University of Wisconsin, Madison, to take over temporarily some of the same courses as my teachers, if I had done anything as ridiculous as delivering their lectures in their absence, it would have been disastrous. The idea of giving the lecturers of my teachers as my own, however, did not occur to me. However I found myself staying in my office in Sterling Hall, where the sociology department was located, until 2:A.M. almost very morning in order to have sufficient lecture material to get through the next day.

When I eventually came to the task of reviewing the major career stages of the college professor, the time period in which his work was under the domination of his doctoral advisor appeared as a distinct phase.[1] Every professor, to be sure, is subject to a number of pressures which vary somewhat by career stage: teaching, service to his department and university; service to the community; professional service, writing and research. If one takes activities of the professor after completion of the Ph.D. for a reference point, all careers have an early, middle, and late phase, often dominated by teaching, writing and research, and service respectively. If one assumes that the Ph.D. is earned by age 28, the first six to seven years are often dominated by establishing one's self as a teacher and earning tenure; the next seven years may be dominated by the writing and research that determine how high the individual will rise in the profession; by his early forties, the time of the professorial mid-life crisis, an individual must reconcile himself to the fact that he has probably reached his peak in the profession. Since only a few reach the top, most professors must come to terms with something less. The mid-life crisis of academic men comes when they realize that they have reached their peak and will never rise higher. They often respond by divorcing their wives to marry a student (becoming a retread) and aspiring to a chairmanship or deanship (substituting service for scholarship as a major life goal). After fifty most scholars are in decline, others want their administrative positions and the market for elder statesmen is not brisk. The ideal type career of the academic man in the research institutions (in contrast to the teaching institutions without major graduate programs and at best minor emphasis on research and writing) can not unfairly be reduced to three:

Career States	Usual Age Range
I: Establishment	Ages 30 to 35
II: Writing, Research and Professional Phase	Ages 35 to 42
III. Service and Administrative Phase	Ages 42 to 50

This, of course, is an ideal type. Many persons never move beyond stage I. Individuals in the teaching institutions have only minor opportunities to participate in stage II, but when they rise in their local contexts it is between stages I and III. Some few scholars in the research institutions manage to scale the heights and their careers are dominated throughout by writing, research, and activity in the profession.

The number of career stages one distinguishes are, of course, matters of convenience and a good case could be made for extending the typical number of stages to five. So many graduate students go forth to accept permanent full time teaching jobs that this could be visualized as the first stage and a case could be made for treating the period from age fifty to retirement as a separate career stage. To individuals who begin teaching before completing their degrees, relations to their academic advisors take on new dimensions. While in his home university the individual is a mere student, in his new university he is a professorial equal to his old adviser (he may even be tenured). However, he is usually not certified to take on graduate advisees of his own until he has completed the degree.

It is essential to take account of the career phase of the academic man in the institution of higher learning, if one is to arrive at a fair appraisal of the ex-advisee as a colleague. Teacher and student move from a one-sided relation of power dependency to one of status equality. The advising relationship may overlap the career stages of both teacher and student resulting in numerous complications.

The type of advising relationship has already been considered in which the student has gone forth and settled into his permanent nitch, but is forced to return to complete the degree to keep his job. More often than not in such cases the student has already permanently settled down at stage one of the professorial career. And, as already observed, the student wants no more from his home department and advisor than the degree which has primarily a negative or defensive meaning in his life. Obtaining the degree under such circumstances primarily represents an unrewarding struggle: long hours of lonely scholarly work, reduced income because the individual has to take time off, and interruption of his family and social life. He is relieved when the torture is over and wishes only to forget the unpleasant experience as fast as possible. While he may retain latent friendly feelings towards him, the advisor is quickly forgotten. Once time has erased the memory of the last unpleasant ordeal, he may begin to feel some nostalgia toward his old department and advisor.

A somewhat happier outcome can be expected from an advising relationship in which the individual seeks to complete the dissertation before entering the job market or when he hopes to reenter the job market to improve his professional situation.

In any superior-subordinate relationship, the question may be raised as to what each party can contribute and can hope to get out of the relationship. There are ancient traditions in all of the major world areas, which elevate the teacher-student relation to the status of an intrinsic value. In fact, whenever the teacher-student relation is formulated in the strict terms of exchange theory (i.e. conceived on a rational economic model as a calculated scheme of value trade-offs) it is headed for trouble.[2] While some teacher-advisors expect to profit directly from the student's ideas and work, most do not. In fact, if any advisor seriously asks whether he will ever get as much out of a student as he puts into him, he will probably never take the advisee on at all.[3] The advisor usually has a considerable range of academic and professional values under his control. The advisee has little to offer in return other than appreciation and loyalty. To be sure, the advisor may find some psychological rewards: reassurance at the presence of a cheering section for his ideas (but if he looks carefully he often discovers that while he is flattered to his face he is criticized behind his back) and a sense of well being at the notion of having a "following" (but he may find to his dismay that many of his "loyal" followers are parasites).

The basic test of the quality of the advising relationship comes during the first phase of the student's own teaching career. Most advisors who do not have an exploitive attitude to the relationship still have a general expectation that some loyalty and friendliness will continue on the part of the ex-advisee when he pursues his own career. He will recommend advisors' books and assign them as texts. He will send on promising students to major in his home department and possibly with his old mentor.

Some of my advisees did in fact use some of my books in their classes, at least for a year or two. A surprising number, however, took care never to mention my books to their students, but employed them as ponys for their own lectures. They assigned as texts the works of other scholars. Far from helping the sale of my books they were taking strategic actions to hurt it. In the long run this tends also to hurt opportunities for further publication by a former advisor, for publishers are not interested in books which do not sell well.

Also, in some of the writings of ex-advisees an interesting device often made its appearance. Basic ideas were taken from my lectures and publications, but they were formulated in disguised form and footnoting was made to other scholars. Many advisees, it seemed, were prepared to go to considerable length to disguise the extent of their dependence on former advisors. I assume that this is something that tends to occur in almost all advisor-advisee relationships except in those cases where the advisor has such overpowering charisma that it is in the interest of the advisee to maximize rather than to minimize his ties to his former patron. In any case, when these practices made their appearance, they came as no surprise, for I had already noted the shrewdness with which some advisees disguised the amount of help they had received on their dissertations and publications that resulted from them even while apparently generously acknowledging aid. The device was simple: all one had to do was to write flowery and emotionally expansive acknowledgements to dozens of people who had contributed virtually nothing to the research and writing and bury among them acknowledgement to the few persons who had been of fundamental and indispensable help.

As these experiences began to unfold, I realized that the Ph.D. is an experimental laboratory of human social relations. Long before some of the negative after-effects of advising had begun to appear, one could anticipate them if one only kept one's eyes open. In the critical phase of a graduate student's work he was under such high tension that his strengths and weaknesses emerged in clear perspective. The adviser who gave much and received only empty flattery for his pains was deceived by this only if he had a will to self-deception. Otherwise, he was made uneasy by flattery for he realized how quickly it could turn into denunciation.

It was, of course, unnerving to have some former advisees for whom one had given unstinting aid, repeat one's lectures and advice as their own,—imitation it is said is the sincerest form of flattery—seek to keep other students from advising with one, decline to use one's book as texts while assigning the books of rivals, and use one's books as ponys for personal lectures. Former advisees who operated in this manner were not so much determined to repay assistance by as much professional damage as possible as taking advantage of a good thing while it lasted.

Some of the persons who seek a professor out as an advisor have a self-seeking exploitive attitude toward life generally. They seize upon an advisor as a bonanza and are inclined to pillage everything in sight. To expect them to do otherwise is to expect the leopard to change his spots. As in life generally, the only sensible attitude toward such types is to identify them early and be on guard. Some of the exploitive types have sufficient native ability to create on their own, but somewhere along the line have developed a basic personality that makes it easier and more attractive to them to thrive by theft than by hard work.

Other persons who continue to pillage ex-advisors into their own professional careers simply do not have the native ability to live in any other way. They have sufficient ability or cunning to work their way through the system and obtain the Ph.D., but not sufficient ability to operate autonomously on their own at the highest professional level. For them exploitation is not a personality inclination, but a survival expedient. Advisors who weep at the ingratitude of such parasitic types of former advisees are deserving only of contempt, for they are continuing to waste energy and emotion over persons who were not worthy of it in the first place.

However, to expect an advisor to recognize the clever and stupid exploitive types in advance and avoid or get rid of them is to ignore the endless complexities of human types and situations. Many individuals who seem promising, never become anything other than promising. Others who seem marginal only blossom when they achieve full professional standing. The stronger, the more creative and autonomous an advisee, the more he tends to evolve into a free and affectionate friend for life. If an advisor will only see it that way, time has a way of shearing off former advisees who are not worthy of colleagueship.

To turn to some specific cases, a distinctive new note entered the letters of two of my advisees at the moment their dissertations, into which I had put much work' thought, and criticism, were published in monograph form. They wrote: "Martindale will not be an unknown for long since he has such eminent students." I thought at first this was meant to be a joke, but it was repeated a number of times under circumstances that left no doubt of their seriousness. Alas, to this day I am still an unknown and waiting, it seems in vain, for a piggy-back ride to fame.

Another advisee into whose work I had put much work and thought and who published his dissertation in monographic form, largely on the basis of contracts with a publisher I had made for him, was so inflamed by ambition with this success that he immediately asked me for suggestions for additional projects. I pointed out that I had advised a number of studies of ethnic communities which had cut new ground. I suggested that it was quite possible that a publisher could be found for an edited collection of such studies if they were well written and carefully edited. I suggested, somewhat after the model of *Old World Traits Transplanted,* by Park and Miller, that perhaps a good title for such a collection was *Transplanted Worlds,* since their book would deal with communities rather than individuals. I agreed to write a special introductory essay on "The Theory of the Ethnic and Status Community," which I did, and to write a final concluding essay on "The Methodology of Ethnic Community Study," if he could not find someone else to do it.

However, I found myself continually badgered to supply ideas and rewrite every line of his text, with never a thought of asking me to joint author the work nor willingness to take into account the fact that he now had a Ph.D. and a published monograph to his credit. Eventually, I explained to him: "You are a big boy now, and if you expect someone to rewrite your material you should invite him to be joint editor with you." This he did, however, not inviting me to join him but asking another student.

Also John Sirjamaki, who was a member of the department at the time, told me that my former advisee came to him inviting him to join the project and stating that "Martindale is trying to hog all the exciting parts of it."

Sirjamaki told me that he asked with respect to the invitation to join the project, "But what does Martindale think of this?" And the former student had replied contemptuously, "Don't worry about it, I know Martindale." When I heard about this from Sirjamaki, I immediately withdrew the essay on "The Theory of the Ethnic and Status Community" I had written for the collection. For some years after this, I heard repeated stories of vicious criticism of me by this particular ex-advisee.

In one instance, a former advisee demonstrated how far he was prepared to go to demonstrate the folly on the part of an advisor in extending himself for an advisee. He had always disturbed me a bit because he was too flattering and I had the suspicion that he thought I was easily "manipulated." Also at times I worried whether he was as competent as he represented himself. The first time I brought him up for his preliminary oral examination he failed; there was no doubt that it was deserved, for his examining committee contained able scholars who leaned over backward to be fair. At the time the privilege of a second try at the examinations was routinely open to all candidates. I insisted upon thorough restudy on all weak points and brought him up again before the same committee. While the candidate performed somewhat better, his performance was still marginal and after long and serious debate the committee decided to pass him inasmuch as I was sponsoring him.

I insisted, after this, that the candidate complete an unusually thorough empirical thesis to resolve any residual doubts as to his qualifications in the minds of his examining committee. I put long hard hours into the process myself, refusing to approve any part of the dissertation until it was, in my opinion, well above a merely acceptable standard. One result of this work was the production of a dissertation that was published as a monograph. I also helped the individual obtain a respectable teaching job.

Sometime after the man was in the field, one of my current advisees came to me with a letter he had received from the former students. In the letter my ex-advisee was seeking to persuade him not to major with me on the grounds that "Martindale is insane." I humbly realized that the individual's preliminary examination committee had, long before, perceived his limitations more clearly than I.

Some of the factors involved in the alienation of advisor and advisee became clear to me only as my own professional career unfolded together with the unfolding of the careers of my doctoral advisees. Former students who never advanced beyond the first stage, who settled into comfortable jobs in which they were inclined to remain for life, tended to retain a kind of sentimental tie with me as their old advisor, perhaps exchanging Christmas cards once a year.

The movement toward rejection, together with pillage and antagonism, tended to characterize some former advisees who were seeking to negotiate the ascent to Stages II (intermediate success) and III (the top) of the academic career. A process could be set in motion that had considerable similarities to the Oedipal drama. To some extent the pillage and denunciation of a former teacher was a kind of bankruptcy proceeding: it cancelled all debts permitting the former student to go on from the relationship with anything he could salvage from it and exclusively his own. Moreover, in academic life as in other areas of American life, individuals tend to measure their own successes in terms of how far they are able to go beyond their advisors as surrogate fathers.

However, when forward motion stalls or when a former student reaches a higher stage in the ideal professorial career, if the break and alienation has not gone so far as to be irreparable, there is at times an effort to restore relations with the old advisor. Meanwhile, the days when an advisor's lectures and wisdom were taken over in their entirety have long gone. In time ex-advisees, who once borrowed freely, gradually acquired in their own lectures a new integration, emphasis and even content. And, in a sense, it does not usually matter any more whether an ex-advisee is repeating his former teacher's lectures or not, for the advisor will have long since modified his lectures into something quite different than they were at the time an advisee had taken his classes.

Of the 73 doctoral advisees, who took their work under me as of this writing, it is my general estimate that half of them are indifferent or antagonistic to me about half remain friendly. At the one extreme are those persons who will not answer letters if they are written to them or even respond to Christmas cards; at the other, persons whose friendship has grown richer over the years and with whom, I am convinced, I will remain friends until we die.

Notes

1. Don Martindale, "Sociology's Students and Teachers," *International Journal of Contemporary Sociology*, 13, No. 374 (July and October 1976), 183-208.

2. Bernard Berelson, *Graduate Education in the United States* (New York: McGraw-Hill, 1960), p. 153.

3. Warren O. Hagstrom, *The Scientific Community* (New York: Basic Books, 1965), p. 1-4.

CHAPTER VI

ON BEING REVIEWED BY A FORMER ADVISEE

Sometimes fate delivers a small part of an advisor's career into the hands of a former advisee. This occurs, for example, when the advisee receives one of his former sponsor's books to review.

In higher education any given cohort of graduate students constitutes a "now" generation. They respond strongly to fads of the moment. Their professors, who were there before them and remain after them, have too many commitments to move more than a few degrees in the direction of the passing fads. In the early 1950s, laboratory experimentation was the latest fad to hit the Minnesota sociology department. The older professors of the department responded to this fad with a shrug of resignation, but they had no intention of directing dissertations in the area. Although some of the younger professors were recruiting advisees, it was to work on projects of their own choosing. By default, as the theorist in the department, I found myself under considerable pressure to accept advisees who wished to climb aboard this latest positivistic-scientific trend.

Though I knew it meant the necessity of working up of the recent experimental literature in post-war social psychology, I was interested in the possibilities of laboratory experimentation in Sociology. In the early 1950s I directed a number of Plan A Master's degrees. The experimental theses included: Richard Marc Emerson's "Deviation and Rejection: an Experimental Replication" (1952); Warren O. Hagstrom's "A Study of the Relationship Between Personality Adjustment and Conformity to Experimentally Developed Perceptual Norms" (1954); Harland Sanford Mickelson's "An

Examination of the Experiment of Muzafer Sherif on the Formation of Social Norms" (1955); and Keith Arthur Lovald's "Submission to Social Influence in Provisional Groups" (1955). This sequence of theses culminated in Richard Emerson's Ph.D. dissertation, "Submission to Social Influence in Face to Face Groups" (1955). By this time the fad of experimental studies was on the wane: Warren Hagstrom was called to military service and continued his academic work toward the Ph.D. at another university; Mickelson had developed an interest in criminology and changed advisors to George Vold, the expert in deviance; Lovald, had developed an interest in the community formation of homeless men.

During the direction of these M.A. theses, I had been working ahead with Emerson in designing an experiment for his Ph.D. I had come to the conclusion that it was impossible to run an experimental procedure adequately on his problem unless he had an assistant to help record data and to introduce "experimental manipulations" at the proper time. But there was no money to hire an assistant, hence I had formed a team out of the various persons interested in doing experimental studies. This supplied the manpower to run each other's experiments efficiently; it also had a kind of chain effect training students on each other's projects. In return for their assistance, Emerson agreed to permit other students to use the experimental equipment he was designing for his own project. Thus Warren Hagstrom became Emerson's assistant and was partly trained on his project; some other student, either Mickelson or Lovald, in turn, trained on Hagstrom's project, and so on.

Though Warren Hagstrom left the campus for two year's military service and never returned, deciding, rather, to pursue the Ph.D. elsewhere, he remained friendly. I heard from him from time-to-time and usually exchanged Christmas cards with him. When in 1960 my *Nature and Types of Sociological Theory* appeared. I received a special note of appreciation from him in which he observed that the book was certain to cause considerable embarrassment in some quarters, for it would make clear where some former Minnesota students were getting ideas for their lectures. This comment could only have meant that Hagstrom knew that some former students were giving my lectures second hand.

Warren Hagstrom proved to be an able scholar, publishing in the area of the sociology of science and developing a speciality in the sociology of the professions. He eventually received an appointment at the University of Wisconsin and moved into the chairmanship of the department. In *The Wisconsin Sociologist* Hagstrom reviewed *The Romance of a Profession* in which I worked up the history of the Minnesota sociology department and told in some detail the problems of several graduate students and of my attempts to defend them. Hagstrom's review is as follows:

> Martindale has written a history of the Department of Sociology at the University of Minnesota from its origins in the first decade of this century to the present. For almost half this period (1921-1951) the department was headed by F. Stuart Chapin, whose character and accomplishments are discussed with sympathy and candor. Chapin's leadership covered two fairly distinct periods. The twenties are characterized as the "golden age" of Minnesota sociology, when the department included such men as Lundberg, Sorokin, Sutherland, and Zimmerman, who interacted in a pattern of "democratic pluralism" and wrote "broad-gauged, global imaginative" works. The later period is characterized as Chapin's "benevolent dictatorship" during which the department maintained its leading position but turned toward

"experimentalism and grass-roots empiricism". Following Chapin's retirement the department declined in relative quality and has yet to regain its former eminence. Martindale is critical of those he deems responsible for this and characterizes the periods since 1951 as manifesting "anarchism," "the rule of cliques," and "power brokers."

As history this volume will be of interest to those who have had connections with Minnesota sociology and of value to those interested in changing patterns of academic social science more generally. (It may also be valuable for would-be critics and satirists of academia, especially for its treatments of sexual and drinking behavior). I wish Martindale had expanded the volume by including more about the intellectual contributions of those connected with the department, for these are described only very briefly. Martindale tends to be a more judicious historian for the period when he was not a participant observer. His accounts and interpretations of events since 1948 are certain to provoke strong disagreement from other participants, some of whom may feel libeled by his treatment of them. The book goes into considerable detail about controversies involving graduate students (about 70 of the book's 272 pages), and those of us suffering from similar problems are unlikely to appreciate the details or the opportunity to read associated departmental memoranda.

The volume is, I think, less successful as sociology than it is as history. There are some interesting but not entirely persuasive arguments presented about the effects of external events on the department, for example that its initial founding was in part a response to the municipal corruption around 1900 and that its growth in the twenties was in part a response to the agrarian depression of the period. There are also passing treatments of the effects of grantsmanship on the department and the pathologies resulting from increased formalization and specialization in graduate education. But the major sociological defect concerns what might be viewed as the central problem of the book, to account for the relative decline of Minnesota sociology after the departure of Chapin. Martindale's focus on particular personalities leads him to neglect possible general social and cultural factors. To be sure, he does have brief treatments of such structural characteristics as inbreeding, and he discusses the relative merits of heads with more or less permanent tenure and rotating elected chairs (I agree with him that neither is clearly superior). But he does not attempt to provide general explanations for the incidence of departmental factionalism, nor does he consider the possibility that state universities (under some conditions) will respond to organized pressure groups by diverting resources from basic disciplines to allegedly more practical and relevant programs (such as Minnesota's programs in mortuary science, native American studies, or criminal justice studies). Nor does he discuss the possibility that the intellectual commitments of Minnesota sociology may have been, in retrospect, relatively unproductive in light of developments in the larger discipline; commitments to symbolic interactionism in social psychology, to a rigidly formalistic grass-roots (or dust bowl) empiricism, and to peripheral specialties, may well have inhibited the department's ability to attract talented faculty and graduate students. Martindale and the readers of this review might well disagree with the preceding speculations. But then, the major virtues of a case study are to generate theoretically interesting hypotheses. Similar histories should be written for other departments; comparing departments we may gain deeper understanding of them.[1]

Warren Hagstrom's review of *The Romance of a Profession* was the most negative the book had received from any reviewer. Particularly intriguing was his tone of disapproval and begrudging acceptance of the book as history, but condemnation of it as sociology. When a young professor named Priscilla Timper from a small nearby university sent me a copy of the review, I could not resist, in my answer to her, some comment on the reaction by former advisees to their one-time sponsors.

I sent on to George K. Floro, editor of *The Wisconsin Sociologist*, a copy of the Timper letter along with a reply to Warren Hagstrom's review, so that he could send on both to Warren for his rejoinder. Copies of the letter to Timper and of the reply and a rejoinder by Hagstrom which appeared in the next issue of the journal follow.

Letter to Professor Timper

My sincere thanks for sending on your reactions to THE ROMANCE and for the copy of the review by Warren Hagstrom.

Two things give Warren's review especial interest to me: (1) its undertone of strong disapproval of me and its inability to empathize with my point of view (anyone who is compelled by his nature to defend others against institutional injustice must contemplate a brutal and bruising opposition—some of the opposition was noted in the *Romance*. it has continued since its publication); (2) the fact that Warren earned the M.A. under my direction.

There is a curious curvilinear relationship of identification-with and disaffiliation-from advisors on the part of those advisees who go on to the larger scholarly and research institutions (in contrast to those who go into the teaching institutions). I am inclined to attribute this to the operation of two laws of post-advisee behavior:

I. Identification-with an advisor varies monotonically with the strength of the need for his services either materially or psychologically.

Hence identification with an advisor is strong on the part of the young (who need help getting degrees, jobs and access to publication) and on the part of elderly scholars (who at the close of their careers feel cast aside and are in need of some anchorage for their tattered self-esteem).

II. The force for disaffiliation-from a former advisor is the square of the magnitude of a scholar's desire to establish a reputation of his own in direct competition with that of his former advisor.

Hence, the great "put down" of advisors by former advisees is a phenomenon of the advisee's middle years when he stands at the threshold of what he hopes will be his decisive push to "greatness.". If he makes it, with a grand gesture of gracious patronage, he may take his advisor back as a satellite; if he does not he may quietly try to reestablish identification with his old advisor once again as part of the sunet image of what "might have been.

Since I delight in the human drama in all of its forms, I was enchanted with the patronizingly left-handed compliment by Warren to me as an historian, at the very time he was undertaking to put me down as a sociologist.

However, apart from Warren's attitudes toward me—which I attribute to no personal animus (in fact, I thought I could read some embarrassment at what he found himself compelled to do) but to the laws of career ascendency so far as they bear upon post advisor-advisee relationships—what most intrigued me about Warren's review was his total identification with academic victimizers and his complete lack of identification with the victims. What a startling parallel of identification with the slave owner as against the slave; with the Nazi death camp exterminators as against their pathetic victims; of institutional oppressors everywhere as against the oppressed. What other meaning can we read in Warren's statement? "The book goes into considerable detail about controversies involving graduate students (about 70 of the book's 272 pages), and those of us suffering from similar problems are unlikely to appreciate the detail or the opportunity to read associated departmental memoranda."

What a marvelous switch. We are invited to take the point of view of the poor "suffering" oppressors with no consideration for any possible feelings of the oppressed. And are we to read this to mean that the sociology department of the University of Wisconsin has been also misusing students? Surely this cannot mean that Warren's lack of identification with the victims flows from the fact that he has been playing the role of institutional oppressor at Wisconsin? Does he really mean to have us take seriously the notion that it is the system or the structure that is responsible for institutional injustice and is no responsibility of those who employ institutions as instruments of personal advancement and power?

> Poor Warren. I knew him when he had a healthy American sympathy for the underdog that arose with unreflective spontaneity. He was happy then. Is he happy now ?[2]

Also an official reply to Hagstrom was submitted to *The Wisconsin Sociologist:*

> I have always been interested in arguments which excuse individuals for institutional injustice and attribute it to system of structure. In Warren's words: "Martindale's focus on particular personalities leads him to neglect possible general social and cultural factors."
>
> I have noticed that this kind of argument is occasionally made by would-be radicals who are afraid to attack persons in power and who sensibly direct their attack at the instruments at the disposal of the power figures. However, the argument is also occasionally made by conservatives who intend to use the structure or system as an instrument of exploitation and who cleverly divert criticism from themselves to the social structure or system. In fact, systems or structures are never more than conditions or instruments. In an ancient observation, no system is better or worse than the good or evil will with which it used. My one-time friend from long ago, C. Wright Mills, never made the mistake of attributing responsibility for the injustice that may be perpetrated in the name of a structure to the structure alone. He preferred to single out the persons who used or misused it.
>
> Warren bolsters his argument that responsibility for institutional injustice and a declining level of academic achievement *may* be due to structural variables by a smoke screen of *possibilities* that raise more questions

than they settle. He states that I fail "to consider the possibility that state universities (under some conditions) will respond to organized pressure groups by diverting resources from basic disciplines to allegedly more practical and relevant programs."

One can only observe that the University of Wisconsin, Madison has had at least as many relevant programs as Minnesota, nevertheless the members of its sociology department managed to reverse a negative trend in the department's ranking, returning it from 12th to 7th place in the United States. Warren continues with respect to my sins, errors and omissions: "Nor does he discuss the possibility that the intellectual commitments of Minnesota sociology may have been, in retrospect, relatively unproductive in the light of developments in the larger discipline; commitments to symbolic interactionism...to grass roots (or dust bowl) empiricism and to peripheral specialties, may well have inhibited the department's ability to attract talented faculty and graduate students."

In view of the developments in symbolic interactionism by Blumer, Strauss, Shibutani, Goffman and Howard S. Becker in the post war period, how can Warren possibly bring himself to deliver this oracle ? No school was ever hurt by empirical traditions. I am sure that Reuben Hill and other members of the family program, David Ward and John Clark in the deviance program, Robert Fulton in the sociology of death, and George Donohue, C. Eugene Ramsey, and Bert Ellenbogen in rural sociology would be sick at heart to see responsibility for the decline in the deprtment's national rank chalked up to their pursuit of excellence in their specialties. And, in any case, why should Warren formulate it as an either-or.

Finally, I do not think the staff or students at Minnesota are inferior to those of any of the major schools. Rather it was my thesis that a combination of personality variables and accidents unleashed a cycle of negative competition (the destruction of rivals and their students rather than the attempt to outwork and outthink them) which tended to destroy strategic forms of team play, to suppress a sense of responsibility for the whole, and to smother excellence under a blanket of mediocrity.

Don Martindale
University of Minnesota

Hagstrom's rejoinder to Martindale also appeared in the same issue of *The Wisconsin Sociologist*.

Don Martindale is quite correct in chastising me for suggesting that structural explanations of social phenomena will absolve individuals of personal responsibilities. Making such suggestions is an occupational hazard of sociology, and it should be criticized when it occurs. It is embedded both in our theoretical orientations and our methods, which often unnecessarily stress the importance of concealing personal identities. I liked Richard Colvard's discussion of the methodological problem (in his essay in Gideon Sjoberg, ed., *Ethics, Politics, and Social Research* (Schenkman, 1967): "It is not necessary to review details...even of the Eichmann case to call attention to the widespread tendency to claim that politically questionable acts were done under 'others' orders'—or in response to role-expectations deemed central to professional practice..." Having conceded, this, I would reiterate my feeling that the individual characteristics of chairmen and other officials are unlikely to be critically important in the long run (however much they may be a blessing or a curse in the short run).

I think individual differences among reasonably competent chairmen are like individual differences among reasonably competent Renaissance painters: when he looks for the consequences of such differences, the connoisseur looks at such trivia as the ways earlobes are drawn, not the major aspects of composition, color, or subject matter.

Although I feel that emphasis on such theoretical approaches as symbolic interactionism and such "peripheral" specialties as family sociology have negative consequences for departmental prestige, I would not like such judgments to be equated with my own assessments of their inherent importance. The symbolic interactionism of Arnold Rose and S. K. Weinberg, along with Don Martindale's lectures and conversations about sociological theory, were very important in recruiting me to sociology in the early 1950's. (Don Martindale is probably one of the best teachers of sociology anywhere; it was my own sense of modesty that led me to neglect stating this in my initial review.) Family sociology is one of my own teaching interests and an area in which I have written a little. But still: the prestige of the Minnesota department is relatively low despite having perhaps the best family sociology group anywhere. And, pending empirical refutation, I would maintain again that symbolic interactionism in the post-WWII period did not lead to enough significant published empirical research or enough major new theoretical insights to give great prestige to the departments in which it was strong—with notable exceptions, such as labelling theory, in which the Minnesota department was not a pioneer.

The Department of Sociology at the University of Minnesota should be better than it is. (Of course, the same is true of all our departments.) Consideration of its history is valuable in part for suggesting how it got that way and what might be done about it. It would be a mistake, however, to conclude that the situation could be remedied simply by appointing the right chairman, just as it would be a mistake to try to remedy the situation by more aggressively fostering certain theories and specialties simply because they are currently fashionable.

Warren O. Hagstrom
University of Wisconsin-Madison[2]

Some poor writing had slipped by into my reply to Hagstrom which he had either missed or had chosen to ignore in his rejoinder. In any case, my reply to his review seemed to have struck Hagstrom in much the same manner as Mark Twain's Connecticut Yankee—who was hit so hard with a monkey wrench that it knocked him all the way back to the Middle Ages. Moreover, he had quite evidently also read a copy of my letter to Timper. It is the only way to make sense of his rather curious parenthetic statement: "Don Martindale is probably one of the best teachers of sociology anywhere; it was my own sense of modesty that led me to neglect stating this in my initial review." For myself I see no immodesty whatsoever in saying that I had and have great respect for some of my former teachers.

However, after he had back-padaled and made some apologies and appeasing gestures, Hagstrom had once again formulated a distorted version of the theme of *The Romance*. In a letter to the editor of *The Wisconsin Sociologist* I called attention to the stylistic blunder in my reply and addressed myself very briefly to the further distortions contained in the rejoinder.

A good example of Warren's basic consideration is his avoidance of mention of the shockingly bad writing in one sentence of my letter. I had said: "Warren bolsters his argument that responsibility for institutional injustice and a declining level of academic achievement *may* be due to structural variables by a smoke screen of *possibilities* that raise more questions than they settle."

I had obviously not bothered to read my own letter before sending it out, or I would have caught the mixed figure of speech: whatever else one does with arguments, one certainly does not "bolster" them with "smoke screens."

In the course of removing himself from the untenable stand he had taken in his review of *The Romance*, however, Warren once again oversimplifies its thesis. "The Department of Sociology at the University of Minnesota should be better than it is...Consideration of its history is valuable in part for suggesting how it got that way and what might be done about it. It would be a mistake, however, to conclude that the situation could be remedied simply by appointing the right chairman, just as it would be a mistake to try to remedy the situation by more aggressively fostering certain theories and specialties simply because they are currently fashionable."

I did not for a moment suggest in *The Romance* that academic departments that shuffle in purposeless mediocrity would stride in purposeful excellence "simply" as a result of "appointing the right chairman." However, now that Warren has mentioned it, I am inclined to think the chairperson can be rather important. Like the editor of a scientific magazine, the head of a laboratory or the leader of a scientific expedition, the chairperson of an academic department can minimize conflicts, encourage team play, identify creativity and reward achievement.

I wonder where Warren got the idea that a component (to be sure not exclusive) of academic excellence consists in "more aggressively fostering certain theories and specialties" that are "currently fashionable" ? Great academic departments in all areas, not simply sociology, are leaders rather than followers in the cultural fashion industry. As Thoreau would probably have phrased it, they aspire to the role of head monkey. "We worship not the Graces nor the Parcae, but Fashion. She spins and weaves and cuts with full authority. The head monkey at Paris puts on a traveler's cap and all the monkeys in America do the same." (Carl Bode ed., *The Portable Thoreau*. New York: Viking, 1947, p. 280)[4]

Don Martindale
University of Minnesota

In all of this, Warren Hagstrom was simply mistaken in his assertion that the primary theme of *The Romance of A Profession* was to account for the decline in national rating of the Minnesota department of sociology and he was mistaken in assuming that I was attributing exclusive responsibility for events in the department to the personalities of its chairmen. I had traced positive as well as negative trends, and had explored the interrelations of these trends with a multiplicity of factors among which the personalities of the participants were only one. Warren Hagstrom had simply set aside the fact that the policies, practices, and controversies affecting graduate students was taken as a particularly sensitive index to these trends. "The book," he observes, "goes into considerable detail about controversies involving graduate students (about 70 of the book's 272 pages), and those of us suffering from similar problems are unlikely to appreciate the detail or the opportunity to read associated departmental memoranda."

The policies that had come under fire and were a source of the controversies reported in *The Romance* had once been applied to Warren Hagstrom himself when he was a student in the department. How far a one-time advisee may move in his professional career from his one-time advisor is quite clear from his review in which he expresses such distance from and distaste for the problems presented by graduate students and shows no empathy for their predicament He missed, in his review, a major opportunity for irony. It would have been more understandable if he had said: "Why all this to do about graduate students, when so many of them, as any sophisticated teacher knows, have such short memories about the help they receive ? Who does not know that advising graduate students is a thankless job ? Need we go this far to belabor the obvious ?"

Notes

1. Review of *The Romance of a Profession* by Warren O. Hagstrom., *The Wisconsin Sociologist*, 13 (Fall 1976), 125-126.
2. Letter to Professor Priscilla Timper, University of Wisconsin, Stout, October 13, 1976.
3. Reply to Warren Hagstrom and Rejoinder to Martindale, *The Wisconsin Sociologist*, 14 (Winter 1977), 4-5.
4. Letter to the Editor, *The Wisconsin Sociologist*, 14 (Spring-Summer 1977), Nos. 2 and 3, 102-103.

CHAPTER VII

WAYSIDE ADVENTURES

Most professors—though theorists and methodologists are particularly pestered—are occasionally approached by students who are not majoring with them, including students in other departments, for help. In some instances their advisors have sent them in search of help. Many professors honor such requests by suggesting bibliography or clarifying an argument or by untangling a methodological snarl. Once in a while such temporary requests and encounters grow more extensive, though it is good sense to avoid involvement in another professor's problems. My rule has been to avoid anything which I would view as interference if it were done by another professor to or in response to one of my own advisees. When this point is approached by a student seeking outside help I have simply said, "That is a matter which you must clear with your advisor."

Shortly after coming to Minnesota an able undergraduate student named Sidney Peck came into my classes. He soon made himself known along with a Minnesota coed he was courting. Both Sid and Louise indicated that they were interested in doing graduate student work in sociology. However, in the course of inquiries made in Peck's behalf, I found that he had a reputation as a radical and a trouble maker among the elders of the sociology department and it seemed to me that he would be unlikely to receive graduate assistance. I recommended that the Pecks consider pursuing graduate work at the University of Wisconsin where, I thought, they would find my old advisor, Hans Gerth, to be brilliantly suited to their needs. Gerth, in turn, I felt would respond to their sincerity, idealism, and intensity. However, I warned them that when they came to do M.A. and Ph.D.

dissertations under Gerth, they might easily find him overwhelming unless they carefully checked out but remained selective among the many helpful suggestions he was sure to make.

The Pecks and Gerth were instantly fond of one another. They adored him and he found them appreciative and loyal. Since the families of the Pecks were in the Twin Cities and they made frequent visits home, I received regular glowing accounts of Gerth and their progress at the University of Wisconsin, Madison.

However, shortly after they began M.A. work under Gerth I received a frantic visit from them, not because they were getting no help, but getting too much. They were baffled and smothered under suggestions, all of them brilliant. They needed a drink of tap water; Gerth had opened a fire hydrant.

I sat down with them, sorted out all the suggestions Gerth had made, rearranging them, indicating which to take, and which to resist, helping them work out the reasons to give Gerth if he asked for them. Thereafter the Pecks made regular visits from Madison, for shakedown sessions on Gerth's advice. The procedure worked out satisfactorily. Sometime later when I was visiting the Gerths in Madison he took copies of the Pecks' theses down off his shelves to show them to me: "Here," Gerth said with evident satisfaction, "are a couple of theses which you should find interesting."

Peck had learned his lessons well on the M.A. When he came to do the Ph.D. with Gerth he no longer needed to consult me, or, as far as I know, anyone else. He produced a brilliant work that was published as a monograph and went on to a distinguished career in sociology, earning something of a reputation as a radical sociologist.

A second wayside adventure in advising involved George Vold, the distinguished criminologist in the Minnesota department at the time I joined it, and Orville Quackenbush, whose graduate student career had been interrupted by teaching and war service. Quack, as he preferred to be called, returned to the Minnesota campus as an instructor in the early 1950s while he finished the Ph.D.

I had grown very fond of Vold, enjoying his courtly manner, appreciating his old-fashioned integrity, and delighting in his cynicism about "do goodism" and the self-serving pretense that so often disguishes itself as idealism. We often had lunch together, and since Vold's home was in the same direction as mine, I often drove him home from the office. We exchanged hospitality with the Volds and friendship with them deepened as the years went by.

Vold's student Quackenbush was older than I and, although he did not have the degree, he had more teaching experience. He was a droll character. It was bad enough to be saddled with a humorous sounding name like Quackenbush, without being decorated with the given name Orville. He had gotten through childhood with such a combination of names, by humorously reducing them to their most ridiculous form as soon as possible. Call me "Quack" he announced at our first meeting. Quack was a good teacher and able scholar, but he was having trouble completing the dissertation—a kind of difficulty that often occurs when a dissertation is not completed at the proper time.

To my astonishment when the Volds were going away on sabbatical during a spring quarter in the 1950s, Quackenbush came to me and asked permission to advise with me during Vold's absence.

"You don't need a new advisor," I said. "Vold will only be gone spring quarter and part of the summer."

"I don't want to change formal advisors, I just want to advise with someone."

"I can't interfere with one of Vold's advisees in his absence," I persisted. "He is a senior colleague and I respect him."

"I have already asked Vold whether I could advise with you in his absence. He's given me permission."

Quackenbush had, by this time, left me no option but to say what was most on my mind.

"But, Quack, you are older than I am and you have more teaching experience. How can I advise you the way I would a green kid and tell you, for example, 'Quackenbush, that idea is terrible. It stinks; scrap it.'"

With deep relief he said, "But that is exactly what I need and want. I cannot move ahead with Vold, because he treats me like a professional and a full colleague. He will not pry and ask me embarrassing questions. Everytime I try to get up courage to tell him how much I don't know, he treats me like such a gentleman that I lose my nerve. I need someone to push me, to tear my arguments apart, to get to the bottom of the matter and find out why I'm not getting ahead. A youngster has a right not to know a lot of things. I've outlived that stage and do not get the help I need."

Quackenbush was, of course, unquestionably correct. If an individual does not complete the degree when he is young and has the right to be naive and in need of help, he often develops personality claims that will not permit him to seek help and has others impose role expectations on him that prevent it. This is a major reason why delay too long in completing a Ph.D. is often fatal.

Quackenbush took a room in the Midway district of the Twin Cities where he would be close enough to my home for quick conferences. I put him on a schedule which included daily meetings with me during which I ruthlessly tore apart whatever he had written until we obtained something I felt would stand. Each day we planned the next day's work. Quack lived like a monk. And I have never had a student before or since who not only took criticism in good grace, but with gratitude. He completed the entire dissertation in one quarter and when Vold returned Quackenbush presented him with a completed draft of the whole. Vold read it critically and found it only necessary to ask for style corrections. Vold never heard how we had worked in his absence, but at lunch one day he said with evident satisfaction: "Quackenbush is all right. He can turn out decent work when he wants to."

A Third wayside adventure in advising did not even involve a sociologist. Quite out of the blue one day I received a phone call from an individual who I had met very casually a few times at evening gatherings of friends in the humanities. William Ernest asked if he could come to see me. I had known that he had been working toward the Ph.D. under a friend in the humanities, Charles Pride, and had taken a job in a college in a nearby city. I did not know whether he had completed his degree or not. I made an appointment with him and he came to see me at home.

I was startled when Bill Ernest told me that he wished to speak to me about his dissertation. Though I started to protest immediately, he asked me to hear him out. He explained that a mutual friend, who knew that I had directed a considerable number of dissertations, had recommended that he see me. He then proceeded to pour out a troubled story of all the difficulties with his advisor, Charles Pride.

He had, Bill said, originally earned the M.A. under another professor in his department. However, when Pride took over the chairmanship of the department he arbitrarily reassigned all graduate students to himself as advisees. Although eventually the department had rebelled and restored the right of advisees to choose their own advisors, by this time he had become personally committed to Pride and felt he could not break without its being disastrous to their personal relations. Meanwhile, he related, Pride simply would not read his material and, at times, even did not return it. Pride currently had in his possession copies of material which he had not responded to in over a year. I asked Bill Ernest why he did not simply change advisors. He had explored this possibility, but found other professors reluctant to take him on until he had first finished and submitted a dissertation to his current advisor. Finally, he claimed to have some evidence that Charles Pride had his own priorities among his advisees and had decided that another advisee, John Reingold, should be put through the degree first and before Bill Ernest's problems were even considered.

I pointed out that Charlie Pride was a friend of mine and I would not do anything to undercut him and that I was not a specialist in his field. Bill Ernest asked me only to read what he had and give him a judgment on its quality. He had brought along a copy of the materials he had completed and left it with me.

Since my undergraduate majors had been in classical humanities and philosophy and I had completed the M.A. in philosophy and since members of the graduate faculty over the years read many dissertations outside our specialties, it was not a presumptious idea to review his material for possible quality. A good dissertation presents a thesis, argues it logically and marshalls evidence to support it. In considerable measure a dissertation is judged on face value in terms of the evidence it presents. A specialist, to be sure, may be aware of things outside and not even mentioned in a dissertation which are devastating to it. This is the point where an outsider's judgment become risky.

As far as I could tell, Bill Ernest's material was basically sound. It was a study of a European scholar of considerable merit who had been eclipsed by his more famous brother. The material had many of the problems dissertations often display in their early stages: some phases of the argument had to be clarified and tightened: some rearrangement of presentation was clearly necessary for maximum effectiveness, some irrelevancies had to be removed, the style was in general need of improvement. It was, however, potentially a sound dissertation that any advisor in the humanities could be proud of. Bill Ernest was not trying to palm an inferior product off on an advisor who was seeking only to maintain quality control of degree work. I was relieved; it appeared to be another Vold-Quackenbush situation with an inability to communicate across the barriers of equality.

In previous experience with extra-curricular advising the results had worked out happily. Sidney Peck had learned how to operate autonomously on his own with superior results on his Ph.D. and the Pecks and Gerths were life-long, devoted friends. I still recalled the pleasure with which Vold told me about Quackenbush's completed draft. And again the men remained friends for life. To the best of my knowledge neither Gerth nor Vold ever heard of the assistance I had given their advisees. In any case, I had only helped without any intention to harm.

In the course of talking with him about his material, I had become impressed with the sincerity and intelligence of Bill Ernest, and the urgency with which he wanted to complete his work. He obviously did not want to hurt his advisor, Charles Pride; but wanted to retain his friendship. I agreed to help him, but only on the conditions that I remain absolutely anonymous. I had no interest whatsoever in building a reputation for interferring with dissertations outside my field. I did not wish to do anything that would interfere with my friendship with Charles Pride.

Bill Ernest had made his appeal to me in April. From April to July I served, through numerous personal conferences and correspondence, as surrogate advisor to him. He had done the basic research on his project before he appealed to me, hence, it was possible to move rapidly on the dissertation, although occasional discrepancies appeared in the original data forcing me to send him back to them. He was a mature scholar with considerable teaching experience, in fact, with much of the same general properties as Quackenbush. He took all criticism in a mature intelligent manner, insisting on knowing exactly why a given line of advice was given. For my part, I made sure that his argument was logically tight, that irrelevancies were purged, that the evidence was tested and sound, that the style was smooth. Along the way I also, made sure that his thesis title was properly filed with the graduate school and that his final oral committee had been appointed. Finally, I arranged for him to have his copy typed in proper form by a superior typist, on proper paper, and in the number of copies sufficient to meet the requirements of the graduate school.

Once the thesis had been completed in potentially final form we met at a strategy conference to discuss the next step. I pointed out to Bill Ernest that he was now in a position to obtain a reading from his dissertation committee even if his advisor was reluctant. All that was necessary was to register his thesis with the graduate school and deliver copies to his reading committee, including his advisor. If he handled the problem in this manner, however, he could expect some dismay on the part of his advisor, who might well feel upstaged. Besides, he was dependent on his advisor's good will and support when he finally met his final oral committee. I advised against this way of handling the matter.

The more tactful and considerate way of handling the problem was to bring the completed thesis to his advisor and ask for his judgment and his permission to deliver copies to his reading committee. Since most advisors take pride in the work of their advisees and receive credit for putting them through, I anticipated that Charlie Pride would live up to his name and respond positively to it, though perhaps he might be startled at the efficiency of Bill Ernest in completing the degree. However, with virtually no work on his part, his student had completed the dissertation and Charlie Pride would receive credit in his department and the university and appear in the commencement bulletin as having piloted another doctoral candidate through the shoals to successful completion of the Ph.D.

In a week or so after Bill Ernest had delivered his completed dissertation to his advisor, I received a frantic telephone call from him: he was crushed by Pride's response to his dissertation. He asked for an immediate conference concerning it. To Bill Ernest's dismay and to my astonishment, Professor Pride had responded to the completion of the thesis with an outburst of fury. At the time it was delivered to him, Pride had been asked by Bill for permission to also deliver copies to the rest of the reading committee. He flatly refused.

He read it, however, and delivered to Bill many pages of detailed criticism, chiefly over trivial matters—for example, where Bill used one term, Professor Pride suggested a synonym A large number of Pride's criticisms were of questionable value; some made the text worse rather than better. At the same time not a single criticism had been offered about the logic of the thesis, the order of the argument or the quality of the evidence marshalled in its support. I pointed this out to Bill Ernest who was in shock. As his dismay receded, Bill Ernest became enraged.

Once I recovered from the surprise at Charlie Pride's response to Bill Ernest's thesis, I began to see his advising activities in a new light. I had known that his advising of graduates tended to stretch over many years, but I had always been impressed by the warmth of his friendship with his advisees. Charlie Pride's advisees were invited to his dinner parties and to his lake home in summer; they were helpmates when Charlie had special projects, including work around his house. His advisees, in turn, entertained the Prides, had them over, went to concerts and plays with the Prides, and celebrated holidays with them. I asked Bill Ernest how he squared the response to his dissertation with Charlie Pride's friendly socialization over the years.

"That's what I've been trying to tell you," Bill said. "Charlie is Janus headed. I and my family have had wonderful times socializing with the Prides. The same thing is true for all his other advisors. But the moment any one of us raises a question about his dissertation Charlie becomes a goddamned martinet. I could tell you dozens of stories, for we all have problems. Socially relations could not be better, but in the instant any one of us raises that awful topic everything changes. I should have left him long ago, but it was quite clear that Charlie would have viewed it as a betrayal of his friendship."

In the light of Ernests' experience, it was clear that Pride's advisees were being kept in a prolonged state of dependence, to be patronized, on the one hand, and to form a cheering section to Pride's opinions and activities on the other. Far from being speeded through their degrees, they were retained in clientage as long as possible. Instead of being rewarded by assistance in completing their degree work, they were being rewarded by permission to socialize with their advisor and participate as dependents in his concerns. Many of Pride's advisees never managed to complete their degrees at all.

This experience opened up a dimension of graduate advising that, I had hardly dreamed existed. In my own advising I had quite unconsciously been imposing the norms of the Protestant ethic on the advisor-advisee relation in terms of which the advisor undertook the obligation to speed the advisor through the degree at the minimum time compatible with the highest competence. "Real life" had been unconsciously defined as full professional qualification for the career. Hence, I had been viewing as comparative failures my inability, no matter how hard I tried, to speed some advisees through their degrees. No matter what I tried some some persons could not be hurried: two advisees who started with me as new graduate students in 1949 did not complete their Ph.D.s until 1961 and 1963, respectively (one taking 12, the other 14 years in all); an advisee who came as a transfer graduate student from philosophy where he had completed everything except the M.A. came in 1957 or 1958 and did not finish the Ph.D. until 1974 (taking somewhere in the neighborhood of twenty years to complete the Ph.D. from the time he started graduate school, around sixteen of these years in sociology).

From personal experience, thus, I had been well aware of the fact that some advisees were in no hurry to complete their degrees. I had assumed it was a professor's duty to speed advisees on their way. Under the circumstances, it should not have been surprising that some professors would also look at the advisor-advisee relationship as a social condition to be enjoyed for its own sake and to be extended and prolonged rather than to be hurried through and terminated. But why did not the rest of Pride's advisees break with him like Bill Ernest and finish the Ph.D. ?

Advising can provide the occasion for a great richness of social life. Particularly when an advisee was located at a nearby small college in a position where he had obtained tenure, the prolongation of adviseeship could have major values in its own right that counterbalanced salary increments or greater security that may come with the doctorate. Continued work on his doctorate kept the advisee immersed in the events and affairs of the university. If his local college did not have a graduate program, he was at least kept abreast of graduate affairs of his home department. It was even quite possible that an advisee's part-time graduate student status continued to be financed, by invitations to teach in summer school in his home department. In any case, it was emphatically not true that the prolongation of the advising relationship was always and only an evidence of advisor or advisee failure.

As observed earlier, most graduate students do not view their slow progress as distressing and Sharp was led to the view that prolonged part-time work as a graduate student has evolved into an acceptable life style for many young couples. Continuing ties with the university on the part of a teacher in a nearby college, while he is completing his doctorate, has numerous values the student may be reluctant to abandon.[1]

Among other things, Heiss explored graduate student conceptions of the adequacy of departmental provisions for the interchange of ideas between student and faculty. Heiss had taken this as an indication of the degree of success of the various disciplines in providing a sense of community for their doctoral candidates. She found this to vary from 50% in the humanities to around 40% in the hard sciences with sociology about midway (42%) between the two.[2] However, provisions by graduate departments for exchange of ideas between staff and students is, at best, only one dimension of a sense of community. Furthermore, between Professor Pride and his graduate students there was no lack of a sense of community, as well as on the part of Bill Ernest until the time when his restiveness over lack of progress in completion of the doctorate began to place a strain on their relationship. In fact, in view of the tendency for graduate student status to emerge as a fairly satisfactory way of life and the inclination by some faculty members, as illustrated by Charlie Pride, to encourage prolonging of doctoral status, the question could even be raised whether it might not, at times, be a disvalue to make graduate student status especially attractive.

The experience with Bill Ernest and Charlie Pride forced on me realization of oversimplification in my own advising policies. Some advisees had left me because I had pressed them too hard to make progress in their graduate work. And who was to say that in changing advisors and taking longer to go through their experience had not been immeasurably enriched ? At the same time, it was clear that a systematic prolongation of the student in the advising relationship also had its limitations. Only upon completion of the degree was a graduate student in position to act with full professional autonomy. His salary, tenure and promotion were often dependent on completion of his degree. If he had writing and research plans, only with the degree was he in position to devote maximum time to them. I found myself both in sympathy with Charlie Pride's response to what he viewed as Bill Ernest's impetuosity and with Bill Ernest's rage at what he viewed as his advisor's sabotage of his graduate progress.

Although Bill Ernest was inclined to refuse to make the trivial changes in the dissertation demanded by Professor

Pride, I pointed out to him that while this might save him money it could well destroy his case. By completing the dissertation without Professor Pride's permission, Bill had out-maneuvered him. He had, by typing his thesis in final form, presented Pride with an accomplished fact. If he now was intransigent about making changes his advisor demanded, he could lose any advantage he had gained. No advisor should be put into the position where he must respond to a *fait accompli* only to have his advisee then refuse to accept correction of his text. On the other hand, Bill Ernest would be on the side of the angels, if he accepted whatever corrections his advisor made without quibbling over whether they were good or bad. I explained to Bill Ernest, that it was also time to make sure that every step of the interaction between him and Professor Pride was recorded, for it was beginning to look as if proof of what had happened would be required somewhere down the line. Bill Ernest accepted this interpretation. At considerable expense he made the changes that had been demanded in his dissertation without quibbling over them and delivered a revised text to Professor Pride. However, though he again requested permission of Professor Pride to deliver copies of the now corrected dissertation to the reading committee, once again Pride refused. I suggested that it was time for Bill Ernest to write Pride a letter in which he tactfully put his case in writing for future reference. I helped him draft the letter. This was on July 15 of the year in which these events occurred.

> Dear Charlie:
>
> I sense that you feel that I am being somewhat importunate with respect to the completion of my dissertation (an inclination, incidentally, which in some quarters is considered praiseworthy rather than blameworthy), so permit me to explain precisely how the problem appears to me.

The dissertation has hardly ever been absent from my waking thoughts for four years. My family, my general professional standing, and my teaching have suffered from the lack of time devoted to them. And now that I have been promised a salary increase and promotion if I complete the degree, each day that it goes uncompleted costs me money.

I know that you are somewhat disturbed that I put the entire dissertation into final form as a sort of *fait accompli*. However, as I see it you gave me no other choice. I hardly need remind you that I placed into your hands every line of the original drafts. Whatever parts you commented on in the last four years have been incorporated into the thesis, as you have undoubtedly noted. On the other hand, you have had some of the present material for over 12 months without my ever receiving your reaction to it. *All* of the material has been in your possession for varying periods from 6 months to a year. This is to say nothing of material in your hands long before this and which you held so long without response that I abandoned it.

As time went by and I despaired of ever receiving your reactions, I came to the conclusion that there was no other course *if* I were to "get a reading" than to make every conceivable scholarly revision of the rough draft and to put the material into final form. It has cost $286.00 to have the dissertation typed into its present form.

Now that I have received your reactions to the text, I have at no time quibbled over your criticisms and comments but, wherever possible, have revised the text to take them into account. Inasmuch as each page that must be revised and retyped represents an additional cost of anywhere from .75 to $1.00 I trust that you will forgive me if I have tried to carry out the revisions economically. It is my dissertation, a product of my labor and my imagination. I am prepared to stand back of it.

When we talked on the phone on Thursday, July 13, you informed me that you had not yet read my final chapter. If your comments on it are ready for me on Monday, July 17, as you promised, I will willingly and promptly make any revisions suggested just as I have done with your previous comments.

It seems to me under all these circumstances I have a right to request a reading by my entire reading committee before the summer is over. You have read the thesis and I have corrected the text in terms of all your criticism. Hence, I feel you should now be prepared to sign the report of the reading committee. I should like to report to my home department that my final oral has been held before September. I realize that you are leaving town soon and this does not permit much time. I might also note that you only cared to inform me of your imminent departure a few days ago. Your suggestion that I send material to your out-of-town address is completely unacceptable. When I followed this suggestion and sent material to you two years ago, I did not even receive an answer.

I believe that I have acted in this matter in the only way possible to move it toward a conclusion. And if you are still not prepared to sign the reading report form and to permit the dissertation to go on to the reading committee, I propose to appeal to the dean of the graduate school for a new advisor.

I trust you realize that my appreciation of your high talents and the numerous acts of generosity extended to me in your former capacity as chairman of the department are in no way dimmed by the present circumstances. But I and my family have suffered long enough over the dissertation and it is high time to bring it to a conclusion.

Respectfully yours,
/s/ Bill Ernest

However, Professor Pride was whipped to greater fury by this turn of affairs. He not only refused to accept the thesis and permit its delivery to members of the reading committee, but actually began to change Bill Ernest's final oral committee to put persons on it whom he felt would back him up against Ernest. I advised that it was time for Bill Ernest to appeal to the new chairman of the department to obtain his permission to serve as his sole or joint thesis advisor. (Bill Ernest had, on my advice, long before this approached the chairman, and in confidence told him the story of what was happening. He had obtained the chairman's permission ultimately to shift advisors if he were not able to sort things out with Professor Pride. The new chairman, for his part, had expressed sympathy for Ernest's predicament, but had wisely pointed out the fact that things would be better for everyone concerned, if Bill were able to work things out with Pride. This request was again made in writing. The new chairman agreed to read the thesis and sit on the committee, but indicated that it was not appropriate for him to ask the graduate school for the substitution of himself as advisor—this request had to come from Bill Ernest. This left the issue squarely up to Bill, to appeal his case to the dean of the graduate school. I helped him compose the letter, taking care to keep its tone professional and making no frivolous charges against anyone. The letter identified Bill Ernest, summarized the events and requested the dean to appoint a new advisor. The letter read in part:

> The dissertation was completed, registered with the Graduate School in June and delivered to Dr. Pride. I asked his permission to give copies to other members of the reading committee, but he was opposed to it. He worked up sixteen pages of criticism of the draft, the overwhelming consisting of minor matters of word usage, phrasing and the like. Since it was not my intention to present either him or any other member of the department with a *fait accompli* on a take it or leave it basis, I proposed to make all changes suggested. I did however resist his suggestion that I make various piecemeal changes checking with him over each one, hence providing further occasions for endless delays. Professor Pride for his part angrily stated on the phone that he was considering writing me a letter.
>
> Thus when I revised the thesis in the light of his comments I prepared a letter of my own for him, indicating that I wished only his approval or disapproval and permission to send the thesis to the reading committee. On the advice of other department members I waited until now before appealing to you for a new advisor. Dr. Pride has now rejected the dissertation in its present form.
>
> I trust that you realize that I am appealing to you for a new advisor only as a last step because all attempts to settle this issue have failed. If you would be kind enough to appoint Dr. Wolf or have someone in the department designated as my new advisor, it might permit me to terminate this matter by the end of the second Summer Session.

In response to this letter and on the basis of his own inquiries into the situation Dean John Milton of the graduate school wrote an unusually graceful letter in which he tried to pour oil on troubled waters and to smooth over the situation and to spare the feelings of all persons involved. The dean wrote:

Dear Mr. Ernest:

With regard to your letter and telephone call, and your difficulties with your thesis, let me say first of all that it is entirely proper for you to have come to the Graduate Dean to consult concerning these—or any other—difficulties which you encounter. I not infrequently wish that more graduate students appreciated the fact that part of the function of the Graduate Dean's office is to assist students when they run into difficulties, and particularly to attempt to resolve the inevitable frictions which will occur between students and the Graduate Faculty. Graduate study is intrinsically a difficult and demanding pursuit, taxing those concerned to the limits of their intellectual abilities, and it is therefore not surprising that strains and difficulties develop.

Next let me point out that it is and has always been the policy of the Graduate School that, since the relation between a student and his adviser involves such a strong personal interaction, both should feel free to sever and change this relationship at any time. It is therefore perfectly proper for you to wish to change your thesis adviser, on the simple basis that your personal relations with Professor Pride have deteriorated—and this need not necessarily imply any criticism of either him or you. Likewise, it is entirely proper and appropriate for an adviser to decide not to continue working with an individual student—and again this need not necessarily imply adverse judgment on the student. You will also understand that in light of this philosophy and policy, the Graduate School would never "assign" either a student to a particular adviser, nor an adviser to a particular student.

In your particular case, I have talked with Professor Wolf and also with Professor Pride, and it is clear to me that you and Professor Pride have reached a stage where you would be uncomfortable continuing to work together in the student-adviser relationship. Professor Wolf informs me that he and a couple of his colleagues are willing to act as co-advisers to you as you move forward with the revision and perfection of your thesis. I see no reason why this should not provide a way of solution to your present difficulties. As far as the Graduate School is concerned, when next you register you should ask Professor Wolf or one of his co-advisers to sign in the adviser's spot on your registration. And it would be useful if you filed a request with the Graduate School, countersigned by your new co-advisers, indicating that you are changing advisers and requesting that an appropriate change in your examining committee be made.

It is of course obvious that you will not be able to complete the requirements for your degree during this summer, which indeed is coming to a close fairly soon. However, from all that I have gathered I see no reason why with reasonable diligence and activity on your part, you should not complete these requirements rather early in the coming academic year. Let me say that if it would be helpful to you in your relations with your dean and the administration of Kingston College, I could readily write a letter to your dean stating these points.

Let me add one more piece of unofficial advice, prefacing it with the remark that in my experience it always comes to pass as a thesis approaches its final stages the student and the advisor require a distaste for one another, sometimes quite mild and sometimes even bitter, but always temporary. There is evident, in the letters and the conversations I have had, a mutual respect between you and Professor Pride for each other's abilities. Do not allow the present situation to obscure your respect for Professor Pride's scholarly ability, nor to cause you to forget the contributions he has made up to the present time to your intellectual development and your thesis study.

Sincerely yours,

John Milton
Dean

Once Bill Ernest's dissertation had been submitted to his new advisors and readers, events moved speedily and happily to a conclusion. He had, of course, to accept and make changes required by his new advisors. Once again they had no criticism of his thesis plan, organization and use of evidence. All changes required were stylistic. Ironically, almost all changes were directed against the revisions made in response to Dr. Pride's criticisms. Bill Ernest was required to put his thesis back into almost the identical form in which it had been submitted to Charlie Pride in the first place.

These events were a source of deep distress to me. What should have been a happy occasion had evolved into a situation of deep trauma for the persons involved. Bill Ernest and Charles Pride deserved to be life-long friends. However, rather than end this chapter on a sad, or, at least a bittersweet note, there were at least two other wayside adventures in advising that had a happier outcome.

In the late 1960s two young scholars joined the Minnesota staff before completing their dissertations. Both were mature, able and promising. William Zwerman and Roy Rickson were completing their Ph.D.'s at the University of Oregon and the University of Washington, respectively. Both had been informed at the time they were hired that consideration for tenure depended upon their completion of their dissertations. Both had experienced the typical delay in thesis plans that attends the need to spend virtually full time on teaching until a person gets his feet on the ground (usually the first year) at a new institution. Both typically, found that when they tried to pick up correspondence with advisors by mail after long delays, progress was slow and erratic. Both eventually appealed to me for help with stories of year-long delays in the answering of correspondence from their home schools and with an increasing sense of alarm as the deadlines for the completion of their work rushed down upon them.

Long before this I had come to realize that the complaints by an advisee who had gone out on a job of year-long delays in the answering of queries or in the response to dissertation material, were not always the advisor's fault alone. My own advisees had often avoided contact with me even when they were still in town for periods that should have given them ample time to complete a dissertation. Moreover they had failed to respond to telephone calls or letters inquiring after their progress. At the same time, I had, on occasion, sudden phone calls or letters or the urgent delivery of material after three or four years of silence accompanied by the preemptory demands of an immediate response to untidy assemblages of material.

Furthermore, forcing an advisor to respond to writing to dissertation material placed an unusual burden on him. A person-to-person conference of an hour or so can cover a lot of ground. Questions could be asked and possibilities explored. To cover the same ground as a face-to-face conference, a full written response could well require a work day or two. To an advisor with a research and writing program of his own, advising in absentia represents a heavy additional burden. Besides, many advisors reason, when they have not heard from the candidate for a year or so, he should not expect a response in less than a year or so. Many an advisee, in short, deems it outrageous to have his advisor treat him in the same manner as he has treated his advisor.

I agreed to serve as a surrogate advisor to Bill Zwerman and Roy Rickson, but, in both cases, urged them to clear up with their home advisors the fact that they were using me as a substitute advisor. This was to avoid possibility of a repetition of the unfortunate events between Bill Ernest and Professor Charles Pride. To the best of my knowledge, this was done and, I believe, accepted with welcome relief in their home departments. In any case I advised both young scholars in much the same manner I had once advised Quackenbush. In this case, however, I urged them to keep sending in material to their advisors as it was finished. However, I proposed that rather than wait until they heard from their home advisors tkey keep the dissertations moving toward a conclusion. If their advisors saw any problem emerging they were quite free at any time to write and ask for changes; if not, and they delayed responding to the material, this would not hold up progress.

Both Zwerman and Rickson finished their Ph.D. dissertations in good time. Zwerman was able to publish his dissertation as a monograph.[3] He was granted tenure at the University of Minnesota, but he was soon lured away to an excellent position at the University of Calgary, Canada. Although Rickson was not as fortunate in obtaining tenure, he was able to obtain a large research grant to study the environmental impact of pollution control and after a few years in the Minnesota Institute of Agriculture, departed for a major academic position in Australia.[4]

Notes

1. See Laure M. Sharp, *Edncation and Employment: The Early Careers of College Gradnates* (Baltimore: The Johns Hopkins Press, 1970), p. 27.

2. Ann Heiss, *Challenges to Graduate Schools* (San Francisco: Jossey-Bass, 1970), p. 155.

3. William L. Zwerman, *New Perspectives on Organization Theory: An Empirical Reconsideration of the Marxian and Classical Analyses* (Wesport, Connecticut: Greenwood, 1970).

4. Don Martindale, *The Romance of a Profession* (St. Paul, Minn.: Windflower, 1976), p. 128.

CHAPTER VIII

ON MALE ADVISORS AND FEMALE ADVISEES

When Sibley made his study of the education of sociologists in the United States he observed that female Ph.D's in sociology were underrepresented on the staffs of universities and four-year colleges and were found in disproportionately large numbers in subcollege teaching and among those not represented on the labor market. Although women were in the majority of recipients of sociology bachelor's degrees (55%), there was sharp attrition in the numbers of women at each successive stage of training and employment, they received only 14% of the Ph.D.'s in sociology and held only 12% of the positions in universities and four year colleges.[1]

A year after Sibley's study, Jessie Bernard's *Academic Women* appeared.[2] Bernard generalized to American academic life as a whole findings similar to those of Sibley for sociology. The modal academic woman was bright (so far as test intelligence was concerned), from an above average social class background, and with major interest in the humanities. In personality she was compliant and non aggressive. Academic women, Bernard found, form a statistically distinct population and serve in academic institutions with functions outside the strategic positions in the academic market place, positions which are not as productive and prestigeful as those that attract men. Women have been forced to settle for second-rate positions.

Bernard saw academic women in motion toward this special position from high school on. Sixty percent of the boys but only 4 percent of the girls in the upper third of their high school classes enrolled in college. Among college seniors 59 percent of the male "A" students planned to go on to graduate school compared to only 45 percent of the comparable female group. Women received one-third of the master's degrees. Among Woodrow Wilson fellows the attrition rate for women was twice as high as for men. Women held only 10 percent of the Ph.D.'s and a high proportion of women Ph.D.'s were not in academic jobs. In her review of the Bernard book Juanita Kreps took note of the tendency by academic women to visualize an academic career as "a vocation for celibacy," and to grow ambivalent over the question whether a woman could be self-fulfilled without marriage and a home.[3]

Bernard's book, and the discussions it provoked, have a nostalgic sound in retrospect, coming as they did before the counter cultural revolt, the rise of the Women's Liberation Movement, the battle cries of the feminists, the systematic spread of assertiveness training and the like. However, writing in 1970 Ann Heiss found that the situation had not essentially changed since Bernard's study. Another investigator found that of 1,500 persons who held academic rank at Berkeley only 61 were women.[4] Another student reported that of 1,043 faculty at Stanford only 49 were women.[5] Even when the military draft forced academic departments to ease their policies on the admission of female graduate students and when women expressed interest in research, they were led to expect that it would be as assistants or collaborators.[6] It is hardly surprising, therefore, that women participated in the protest movements of the 1960s in disproportionate numbers.[7]

While opportunities for women in higher education are expanding, change is slow. Between 1947 and 1975 the proportion of earned doctor's degrees by women increased only from 12 percent to 21 percent and is expected to reach only 25 percent by 1980.[8]

In the 20 years between 1955-1975 of 73 persons who earned the Ph.D. under my direction 16 were women. Of the women who took Ph.D.'s with me nine were single, seven were married. Two of the single women were nuns. No account of advising could be complete without some consideration of what it was like to advise women through the Ph.D.

Since 16 (nearly 22%) of the 73 doctoral candidates who completed the Ph.D. under my direction were women, I had a fair sample to compare with my male candidates. Furthermore, some women who began advising with me transferred to other advisors or, or had been asked to transfer. One female advisee became furious because I was pressing her to get on with her work. In 1959 or 1960 she transferred to another advisor with the sarcastic observation: "I'm going to transfer to someone I can work with." She is still around the University—as of March 1979—without having completed the Ph.D. Another female advisee was asked to transfer because of repeated bitter criticism of me.) And, finally, since my women advisees were about half married, half unmarried, at various ages (from my own age to very much younger) and even included two nuns in their ranks, they formed, a respectable cross-section of the women who obtained Ph.D.'s from Minnesota in the post-war period.

When I review them as a whole, the most significant thing about my woman advisee is the way they defy the stereotypes. They varied in personality from relatively shy and withdrawn, through, straightforward, to bold and brassy. They included feminine types and tomboys; traditionalists and liberated women. They had much the same range of intelligence and interests as my male advisees. The two most brilliant quantitative sociologists among my advisees were women: one, for reasons of her own, chose not to go beyond the M.A.; the other earned the Ph.D. with a competent laboratory experiment. The single most creative intuitive sociologist among my candidates, on the other hand, was a man.

By and large the progress of my female advisees was subject to the same erratic starts and stops as their male counterparts and for parallel reasons. The two nuns had greatest difficulty in arranging with their orders for sufficient time to complete the routine requirements, but once they started on dissertations they made rapid regular progress— as, indeed, did other candidates whether men or women when their home or domestic situations were stable. Married women working toward Ph.D.'s had their progress powerfully influenced by their home situations. Single women tended to follow an erratic course related to the progress of their love affairs. Like their male counterparts the periods of falling in love and the periods of the breakup of affairs were devastating to progress. The in-between periods tended to be characterized by sustained work.

No one could spend time in coeducational institutions of higher learning without becoming aware of the atmosphere of diffuse eroticism that characterizes so many of its situations. Nor could one for long serve in co-educational teaching situations, even the most humble teaching assistantship, without receiving a variety of sexual signals.[9] It was also clear in the pre-war period that although a revolution in sexual mores was taking place in the wider society, American institutions of higher learning were still strongholds of Victorianism. Inside as well as outside the universities some students of the depth psychologists (particularly Freud), became apostles of, in Marianne Weber's words, "a new social ethics."

Marianne Weber had observed: "Female disciples of this 'new ethics' caricatured chastity as the morality of monks, and marriage as the state's compulsory institution for the protection of private property. They demanded the right to 'free love' and illegitimate children. Young women who had just been freed from the constraint of their families struggled with the new message, and many welcomed it."[10]

Marianne Weber reported that Max Weber was fascinated by Freud, but found himself in reaction to some of the social-ethical rationalizations based on Freudianism which, he felt, promoted moral shoddiness in the name of healthy nerves. Weber was interested in "the effects of a norm-free eroticism upon the total personality,"[11] and fascinated not only by "the strong characters who thrived in the new freedom, but also the profound sufferings of those who were defeated in the erotic struggle."[12] While rejecting the new sex freedom for himself, Weber declined to condemn it in others. On at least one occasion he quietly rejected the sexual invitation of a young woman to whom he had given legal counsel on how to keep her illegitimate child from being taken from her by the state.

By the time I read Marianne Weber's account of the new ethics and Max Weber's reaction to them, I had begun to accumulate personal experiences of invitations to sex of varying degrees of explicitness by students in classes where I was instructing and comparative knowledge of the experiences—or at least reports of the experiences—of others. Max Weber's response were based on a pattern of personality variables and of social and cultural circumstances similar to my own. I was, perhaps, rationalizing my inhibitions by reference to Weber when I found myself taking him as a model. However, I was heartened by Weber's disinclination to condemn in others behavior which he did dot condone in himself and by his refusal to assign moral superiority to himself in the process.

The shift from ordinary student to graduate teaching assistant status could not have occurred for me in better courses than Max Otto's *Logic* and Eliseo Vivas's *Philosophy of Contemporary Literature*. Among the novelists discussed and read in Vivas's course were Dreiser, Proust, Hemmingway, Huxley, and D. H. Lawrence. The course was popular and recruited students from the humanities. They were fascinated by the 20th century novelistic reinterpretation of the battle of the sexes. Students were drawn to the course for stimulation and the insights their readings offered them into their own lives and motivations. Many of the students (particularly the coeds) were not above romanticizing their personal situations by envisioning themselves in the roles of heroes and heroines of the novels. At times the lines between reality and make believe were ambiguous. Students in the Logic course, by contrast, did not move in an equivalent atmosphere of diffuse eroticism. Some courses at universities pander to the unresolved erotic frustrations of students. The content of a course and the manner in which it is taught determine whether it will invite or discourage student eroticism. Logic discouraged it; the Philosophy of Contemporary Literature invited it.

Assisting in the *Philosophy of Contemporary Literature* and *Logic,* not only clarified for me differences between the roles of student and teacher, but contrasts between the world portrayed in the works of contemporary novelists and the world of the American university in the pre-war period. At least in the American Midwest the universities of the 1930s and 1940s were still strongholds of Victorianism. Universities were still expected to serve as parent surrogates for undergraduates. Although there was some sexual experimentation among students and occasional companionate marriages among them, companionate marriage in theory, was still heresy, and companionate marriages in fact, if brought to public attention, could still lead to dismissal from the university. Madison, Wisconsin still remembered the infamous Rocking Chair Incident as it was named from Dean of Men Goodnight's resourcefulness in borrowing a rocking chair from the landlord and remaining all night outside the apartment of a pair of seniors who were living in companionate marriage. The dean nabbed the culprits as they left their apartment in the morning to attend classes. A major scandal erupted when William Ellery Leonard of Wisconsin's English department publicly defended the students and made a case for companionate marriage in the Madison newspapers. The young man and woman were expelled from the university At this time sexual scandal with students could still cost a professor his job.

From the standpoint of some of those who view higher education as an ivory tower remote from the ugly realities of the rest of social life, the world of sexual relations described by the contemporary novelists was "real" while the sexual relations between men and women in American institutions of higher learning were not. In such representations, the term "real" acquires ideological force: it both recognizes a difference between sexual practices inside and outside the universities and undertakes the elimination of the difference. In the Victorian stereotypes, which the novelists were contesting, men and women were assigned different and complementary sexual roles; the man was active and aggressive; the woman passive and defensive. From this point of view man's game was rape; woman's was seduction. Wherever Victorian stereotypes prevail women are neither encouraged or taught how to challenge authority. While they are expected to make themselves attractive, sexual initiative is supposed to come from the man. And many a rape case has been lost because the defence was able to argue successfully that the woman had made herself attractive or available, in short, that she had "asked" for it, had actually seduced the man.

In the pre-war period the majority of coeds still came into the institutions of higher learning from middle class families where they received Victorian upbringings. The masculine-feminine scale on which they were trained to frame their expectations, assigned initiative, imagination and intelligence primarily to men, passivity, faithfulness, and intuition primarily to women The novelists, by contrast, were describing a world of sexual relations that bore little resemblance to such Victorian models D. H. Lawarence, for example, had breath-taking insight into feminine cruelty and violence.

At the time I was coming to the conclusion that higher education in America was a Victorian institution, the world was about to complete my education in another sphere. Soon after the war broke out I was drafted. I eventually went to officer candidate school and was commissioned. I spent the next four years in the Army of the United States. About half of my military service was spent in staff, the rest in line organizations, both in the states and overseas. During this time my father died, leaving me responsible for my mother and four youngest siblings, and I married.

Sexual mores in the civilian and military bureaucracies of military posts, camps and, stations and between soldiers and women in the states and overseas bore little resemblance to the Victorian practices of middle class American families or of American educational institutions. Families and schools of all sorts (including colleges and universities) are socialization institutions; armies are control institutions. In the army sex is incidental and peripheral to the main business. Furthermore a large proportion of the men and women who encounter one another in the course of military life have been temporarily torn out of the contexts of their families, religions and communities—they are outside their traditional systems of control. If there was a rule at all, it seemed to be that all women (whether secretaries, nurses, military personnel, or civilians, whether married or single) were fair game. Prostitutes, both professional and amateur, collected around military establishments—"seagulls who follow the fleet." The chief concern of the military authorities, among whom I found myself when I became an officer, was not to prevent military personnel from exploiting every sexual opportunity that came their way, but to prevent it from exploding in civil or military law suits or resulting in venereal disease with a consequent loss of efficiency.

Among the images of sexual behavior that remain over from military life are: the officers who, though married and with families, set up substitute liasons (often with the wife of an absent war worker or absent military man) as soon as possible near any base where they happened to be stationed; the worried captain in the B. O. Q. (Bachelor Officers' Quarters) mess hall swallowing raw eggs, for he had just received word that his wife was arriving in town later that day and he feared he would not be able to raise an erection and perform his masculine duties because of his torrid sex with his local mistress; the secretary in headquarters who, though married with a husband overseas, set up sexual liasons with newly arriving married officers and who, once the affair was underway, wrote to their wives to tell them about it; the colonel who was transferred to the base, bringing along his entire harem of call-girl secretaries, placing them in good positions on the base and locating them in a house he rented in town—according to the colonel's aides one of his women (the wife of a master sergeant who was serving in the infantry overseas) served as madam of the colonel's establishment, keeping a duty roster to determine which girl was on sexual assignment to the colonel for the night; the general officer on inspection who visited the post and, according to the junior officers charged with arrangements required that call girls supplied for his use each night be chosen according to specifications; the colonel who plotted with his aides to frame the civil service head of a major post operation in order to provide an appropriate job for his mistress; the soldiers who during the ten minute rest stop on a troop train on its way to a port of embarcation still managed to contract V.D.; the anguish of men of any rank overseas when they received "Dear John" letters from fiancees or wives. However, I also noticed during my years in the military that there were always men at all levels who cherished their marriages or commitments to fiancees and remained faithful to them. They were less visible than their sexually emancipated compatriots, but they were always around and it was my impression that they were in the majority.

When I returned to the Wisconsin campus after discharge from the army in 1946 it was soon apparent that while still basically Victorian, the atmosphere of the university had changed. The millions of men and thousands of women who had served in the armed forces or war industries and who were returning to the campuses or entering the university for the first time, brought with them more experience with the ethics of the wider society than the pre-war student population. Moreover, G. I. benefits were expanding the base of class recruitment to the universities, bringing in many students who did not have the conventional upper middle class upbringing so characteristic in the past.

In this more mature, less adolescent atmosphere of the post-war university, I wound up my preliminary examinations and took a position on the circuit of the University of Wisconsin extension division. After one semester on the circuit I was called into residence at Madison to fill in for Howard

P. Becker, who was leaving the campus temporarily for service in the American Army of Occupation in West Germany. I still had to finish the dissertation and only had the rank of acting instructor, but I was assured by T. C. McCormick that the position was potentially permanent.

Soon after I returned to the Wisconsin campus to complete the degree and to teach, an incident occurred which dramatized the extent to which the post-war attitudes toward sex had changed. One of the full professors married a graduate student. Before the war, such an event would have been a minor scandal and the source of much gossip. There was not even a ripple. Furthermore I was surprised by Hans Gerth's response to my comment: "He is so much older than she: What does she see in him?" The comment was actually elicited by the fact that the individual concerned while good looking in a conventional way, had a cold self-seeking personality. Gerth said: "It is a brilliant coup for an adventuress. In one shrewd act she has become the wife of a full professor. Think of the years of struggle that would have to intervene before she arrived at that position if she married another graduate student. And he might not make it at all." Gerth went on to call my attention to the fact that feminine adventurism had become much more common since the war than before it.

In the post-war world the Victorianism of the colleges and universities were beginning to relax. When an adventuress pursued a married professor or a married professor pursued his coeds it was more usually a source of humorous gossip than of moral outrage. When an accidental pregnancy resulted the usual reaction was a hasty divorce and remarriage for the sake of appearances, but usually no loss of position. When a professor suddenly became available, female adventurism was unleashed, as illustrated by the experience of a professor at a nearby university who was widowed by his wife's suicide. He went into shock and deep depression over the event and took a sabbatical and went to live for a time in his parental home to recover from the emotional trauma. One of his women advisees followed him into exile, took an apartment nearby and offered every type of comfort a woman can to a man in distress. Possibly because of the recency of his loss, possibly because she was too importunate the liaison did not end in marriage. Sometime later, however, when teaching duties were assumed, a young woman advisee who had come to the professor's house for a conference and left to catch a bus, later turned up at the door in tears and with the report that she had missed her bus. She was taken in, comforted and ended up staying the night. This was the opening scene in a drama ending with their marriage.

Also in the immediate post-war period, stories began to circulate for the first time of the routine sexual exploitation of female students by members of the faculties of the coastal universities. C. Wright Mills described to Hans Gerth and to me, how when he reported for a job interview at one of the major eastern universities he was picked up at the airport by a famous professor accompanied by two call girls. Mills said they were taken to a restaurant and had been signed into hotel rooms with their women. Mills stated that the position for which he was being interviewed was not even discussed until breakfast the following morning. When Mills was asked whether the stories that sex was routinely expected of the young women who served in the research establishments of the eastern colleges was true, he confirmed it and laughed at the naivete of the question. In fact, it was in answer to this question that he elaborated the story of his job interview.

Student advisees also confirmed Mills's observation. In the 1950s I had a husband-wife team originally from New

York working on simultaneous doctorates. A major problem facing them was the military draft (during the Korean War), for he was being called up by his board. When they reviewed their possible strategy for separation during his war service, they decided that it would be better to return to New York. In this manner she could stay with her parents, but continue her graduate degree work at one of the eastern schools, preferably Columbia. They returned to New York, and she explored the prospects of obtaining some sort of financial assistance and to this end set up an interview with an internationally prominent sociologist associated with the Bureau of Applied Social Research.

However, when her husband failed to pass his army physical examination because of high blood pressure, the job with the bureau was scrapped and the couple returned to Minnesota to complete their degrees. It was then she related her brief experience with the bureau.

She had been very much worried, she explained, because of the rumor rampant among Columbia graduate students, that every female appointee to the bureau was expected sooner or later to go to bed with the professor who had interviewed and hired her. Moreover, she reported that when she had been interviewed, the questions raised had been relatively cryptic and noncommital, but rarely had she been sized up by such calculating eyes. She passed inspection and was hired on the spot.

When she related the events of this interview to other woman graduate students at Columbia, she stated that they laughed at her naivete and said,

"Of course, he expects to go to bed with you."

When she wondered out loud whether she should not refuse to accept the research appointment, they advised,

"Hell! Take the job. When he finally asks you to go to bed, and he will, run like hell."

One sophisticate however added: "That is, of course, if you are not too compromised by that time or if you realize that it doesn't matter anyway."

When in the late 1960s and early 1970s the counter-cultural revolts carried through the last stages of the revolution in sexual morals and the last bastions of Victorianism in the universities began to fall, there was a build up in the numbers of women graduate students who chose me as an advisor. I assumed that in some measure these women were refugees from sexual harassment by other members of the staff, for it was also at this time that the volume of rumors began to swell, rumors to the effect that many advisors believed that the advising relationship brought with it sexual privileges. The midwestern universities, it seemed, were finally catching up to their sophisticated counterparts both East and West.

I never checked out the question whether the increase in the number of my women advisees in the late 1960s and early 1970s was produced by changes in the sex mores and the desire of some young women to complete their degrees on sexually neutral territory. I did not at the time ever anticipate putting together a monograph on doctoral advising such as the present one. I had a long standing rule never to question an advisee, male or female, about his or her sex life. I also avoided priest-like relations with advisees, for the purpose of the doctoral advisor was to create intellectual equals not congregations of the pious and penitent. Whenever I sensed that confessional revelations were about to be blurted out, I discouraged them by a change of topic or termination of the conference. I did not want the kind of information about women or men they might later hate me for possessing.

Although business went on as usual during these years with my own women advisees, the harassment of woman students, both graduate and undergraduate, by some members of the faculty grew more blatant. Eventually a formal protest against sexual harassment was made to the graduate faculty by women graduate students. This eventually led to the proposal for a Sex Exchange Monitoring System which would give female graduate students the right to be left alone if they chose.[13]

The situation at Minnesota which led to the proposal for a Sex Exchange Monitoring System, was not unique. Complaints about sexual harassment were increasingly heard from all parts of the country. In 1977 a new stage was reached when a number of women filed a class action suit against Yale University for maintaining an atmospoere of institutional sexism that encouraged sexual harassment. The suit filed in federal court claimed that the Yale Corporation had ignored complaints of sexual harassment thus discriminating against women on the basis of sex, in violation of Title IX of the Educational Amendments Act.

An updated examination of the Yale suit and review of the problem of sexual harassment in the universities was made by Adrienne Munich for *Psychology Today*.[14] Munich's article "Seduction in Academe" stimulated a series of letters which appeared in the May issue (1978).[15] Munich interviewed Attorney Ann Simon and her sole remaining client (after Yale University had successfully challenged the right of five other women to sue), legal spokesman for Yale, psychiatrists, psychologists, professors, and woman students in review of sexual harassment in the universities.

When Munich asked a professor at Yale Medical School whether there was any substance to the student charge of sexual harassment on the campus, he observed the students report it to be common, and described the practice as "fuck or fail." This, of course, was a humorous student overstatement. A professor who wrote in response to the Munich article and who appears to have permitted no opportunity for sex with students to go unexploited, denied having heard of it, insisting that seduction had no meaning in professor-student relations. At the same time he insisted that he had inavariably found himself in the position of being seduced by female students. Voilence and physical coercion is rare. Usually the professor asks and the student is left to wonder what will happen if the request is denied (one of Munich's informants described the results as psychological coercion). As could be expected student-professor sex relationships are found many degress—from blatant seduction by the student to actual rape by the professor. Sometimes a student is even faced with the prospect of both fuck and fail. A professor with whom I was discussing the Munich article stated that at his home school, one of the California State Universities, one full professor first seduced female students and, later, when he read their papers (in response to their crudeness at assuming they could buy grades with sex) failed them: a practice which had led to explosions from which his colleagues and the university administrators managed to extract him only with the greatest difficulty. The significance of this case is the illustration it provides as to how far the American universities have come from the time when sexual scandals involving students (or the wives of other faculty members) resulted in the loss of positions.

When Munich interviewed one Yale alumnus who is now an attorney for the university, she found him disinclined to take the students' complaint about sexual harassment seriously inasmuch as the same thing happened all the time to secretaries. The attorney, of course, was correct; sexual harassment has always been the lot of the working woman in business offices, hospitals, political and governmental organizations, and, above all show business. And the attorney's comments document his awareness that these practices are now spreading to the universities. However, when the attorney takes the diffusion of the patterns of sexual harassment from non-university to university contexts as a reason for the denial of the student suit, he is not also taking account of the fact that working women are, too, fed up with sexual harassment and increasingly resorting to court action to bring it under control. Feminist organizations such as the Alliance Against Sexual Coercion and Working Women's United Institute have been taking cases of sexual harassment to the courts and one woman, Diane Williams, collected $16,000 in back pay after being fired for rejecting the sexual advances of her Department of Justice boss.

Not all students or ex-students interviewed by Munich, wished to avoid sex with professors. She reports that one woman remembered her professor-lover warmly, insisting that he had influenced her choice of a career and determined the subject of her first book. A Radcliffe alumna viewed her affairs with faculty members as a reward for her superior scholarship. And sometimes students receive more than grades, career help, and direction from their liasons. Munich reported that the middle-aged professor who discards his old wife to renew himself by marrying a student is known in college slang as a "retread." A Cornell professor was quoted to the effect that in virtually every department in which he had served there was at least one retread. In the letters stimulated by the Munich article one young woman complained because her former instructor did not respond to her sexual advances. She stated: "In some cases the alleged atmosphere of abandon on campus is being replaced by near-paranoia, which, in my opinion, isn't any healthier." A professor who wrote in response to the Munich article claimed that both his present and his former wife had been students, suggesting, professor-student relations sometimes result in "treads" as well as "retreads." At a time when enterprising coeds are able to view any married professor as a prospect for a retread, the university can be viewed as an expanding field for female adventurism.

However, Munich amply documented the costs to some students whether they resist or yield to the sexual advances of professors and advisors. Pamela Price, the sole plaintiff left in the Yale law suit claimed that when she delivered a paper for an international-relations course in the spring of 1976 she was told by the professor that she would receive an A if she slept with him. She refused and received a C. Though she twice complained to the administration orally and in writing, she was told nothing could be done. Ronnie Alexander, one of the original Yale plantiffs was only 17 when seduced by her professor. She was so filled with guilt, shame, and remorse as the affair unfolded that she changed her major, but held off until after graduation to bring suit (which made her case moot, resulting in her elimination from the suit). Joyce Seifert of State College, Pennsylvania, stated that she was a naive 22 year old and did not know how to cope with the sexual advances of her professor-advisor. When struggling with the mixed emotions that accompanied the affair her grade point average droppped. When the affair was terminated she found herself so depressed that she left school, managing to pick up the pieces of her life only five years later with the help of a feminist support group. A professional musician who graduated from the New England Conservatory of Music was so overwhelmed by the sexual fantasies and advances of her eminent teacher that it required a year for her to secure a change of teachers and it was ten years before she was able to obtain psychological perspective on the incident.

Eros in the classroom is not new, but public complaints about sexual harassment are. As universities have expanded their opportunities for female adventurism, the pressures on those women who by background or personality are not prepared to participate in the new sexual freedom have grown. On one occasion two women graduate students at Minnesota told me about the gross sexual insult administered to one of the new female graduate students in a seminar. The professor had come to the seminar inebriated. After surveying one of the new graduate students for a while, he asked her publicly: "How many times a week do you fuck?" The girl sat speechless and mortified. The rest of the students shared her embarassment and tried to pass the matter off. For the next two hours, the professor was reported to have made vulgar, insulting remarks to the seminar as a whole. I was asked what I thought of this.

I said the girl should have left the seminar instantly, gone straight to her attorney and told him the entire incident, noting the time, place, circumstances and who was present as a potential witness. It would not, I said, have been necessary to take action, but a record should have been established just in case this, or any other, professor engaged in more real or symbolic acts of sexual aggression.

The graduate students who told me about the incident and asked my opinion about it exclaimed: "But Professor Martindale, you do not understand. Some women do not object to sex with the professors and some are getting good research appointments and career help out of it. Why, one woman is even going to get a book out of it. When some women play along with the system, anyone who does not may be destroyed. And if one protests it is one's word against the professor's and after the protest one may be marked down for destruction. Even a public sexual insult in a seminar could be explained away as an ethnomethodological experiment in the manner of Harold Garfinkle."

Along with the increase of female adventurism in the universities, which weakens the position of those coeds who are not seeking sexual adventures, many, perhaps most, professors have abandoned all pretense of maintaining Victorian interpretations of their responsibilities toward their female charges. Munich observed that to hear some professors tell it, the behavior of their female students amounted to open invitation to sex. In a letter to *Psychology Today* in response to Munich's article, one professor advanced an interesting rationale for his superior sexual attractiveness to coeds.

> With so many virile young men around, why should an intelligent, attractive, and conscientious coed express a more than academic interest in her professor ? The answer isn't simple; there are several possible reasons, most of which I've eventually discovered, usually in retrospect, after the affair. Some women are attracted to older, seemingly wiser, certainly more knowledgeable men; others are on the rebound from broken love affairs; others are primarily interested in achieving status among their peers by "capturing" the professor. Some are experimenting with different partners; some are divorced or older women who find it difficult to relate to the younger students and feel more comfortable with the professor; others think a personal relationship will help their grade; some are really neurotic and in need of a parent figure; and others are simply curious about the sexual prowess of those professors who are always reciting love poems with passionate conviction.

> So you won't think I'm a cynic or a woman-hater, let me add that I believe a genuine love sometimes develops in campus affairs. It happened to me twice, and both

my first and present wife were students of mine. I'm inclined to believe that my five-month-old daughter couldn't care less where and how her parents met.[16]

While male professors have abandoned all notion that young women coming into the university require any special protection from sexual exploitation, it is clear that many of these young women still have essentially Victorian training. Dr Maria Kovacs who was interviewed by Munich, is unquestionably correct in her assumption that the rules governing the behavior of people in power in the university have changed.

If a professor felt that sex with students would hurt his reputation with his colleagues, he might hesitate to act on his desires....In our times, however, personal conduct is increasingly kept separate from professional performance. As long as a professor publishes, his reputation grows and he can feel reasonably secure that his peccadilloes will be ignored by his colleagues.

Professors who have made tenure decisions corroborate Kovacs' observations. One social scientist remembered an instance of a man receiving tenure even though he had slept with the wives of several graduate students. "Although this was common knowledge," he says, "it was not a factor in our decision. The matter was never brought up. We generally go out of our way to avoid comments, favorable or unfavorable, about colleagues' private lives."[17]

Indications appear both in the Munich essay and the letters elicited by it that feminists are moving into the vacuum created by the decline of Victorian norms governing the behavior of professors toward their female charges, while many of these same young women are still provided by their home situations with Victorian cultural upbringings that ill-prepare them for dealing with sexual harassment from persons in authority over them. Sheila Tobias, a feminist associate provost at Wesleyan, thinks it is useless to try to turn back the clock and restore professorial and institutional restraints. She takes the position that coeds have to learn how to take care of themselves, avoiding behavior that could be misconceived as seductive, on the one hand, and responding to unwanted sexual advances from professors by learning to "fight or flee" on the other.

However, despite the brave efforts by feminists to teach women how to avoid or resist sexual harassment in the universities, it can be expected to continue so long as families, religions and local communities train their young women to look at men, particularly at men with reputations in positions of authority, with stars in their eyes, assuming respectful and obedient attitudes toward those in authority. Once the institutional restraints, were withdrawn from the sexual exploitation of their female charges, one could hardly expect professors (who often are immature, adolescent types to begin with no matter how considerable their reputations) not to crowd to the feast. At the same time professors who have sex with numerous coeds, costing some of them five to ten years to straighten out their lives afterward, surely deserve the law suits that some of their "scores" will bring against them. As the threat of lawsuits against professors for sexual harassment grows, one can anticipate a new era of voluntary self-restraint from those professors who view discretion as the better parts of valor.

The problem has never arisen for me since I have always been convinced that sex should not only be confined to consenting adults, but between equals for whom even the hint of real or psychological coercion has been eliminated. However, from the beginning it was clear that advising women doctoral candidates presented special problems. For one thing the personalities of women were usually more complex than those of men; for another sex was somehow or other quietly in attendance at most encounters. Women generally saw more quickly than men, that the attempt was made to maintain relationships on a professional level—and long remained skeptical about it. When it was essential to get to the bottom of a problem, women concealed a weakness longer. Not infrequently a pseudo weakness was offered as a hostage, to conceal a more serious weakness. Women usually appraised social situations more quickly and accurately than their male counterparts. Virtually never did a woman come to a major conference without attending the beauty parlor first. Women dressed skillfully for major confrontations (such as preliminary and oral examinations) and quietly set the stage that made the desired outcome more certain. They generally sensed the undertones in face-to-face situations more quickly than men and responded to them more appropriately.

At the same time I sometimes became aware during a conference with a woman advisee, that a subtle kind of coquetry had crept into the exchange. Intriguing hints and signals appeared that seemed to invite more intimate exchange. Almost never would a woman mention a husband or boyfriend, where it would have been normal for a male advisee to mention a wife or girlfriend. At times, I became aware of the fact that wedding or engagement rings magically vanished from fingers and, occasionally, a sort of atmosphere or nimbus would seem to descend around a female advisee— as if she were enveloped in a cloud of unbelievable innocence and purity, as if any suggestion her advisor made was no less than the wisdom of the ages and she was enthralled by its deathless insight. At such ecstatic moments I was reminded of Nietzsche's observation: "When love is not involved, woman's game is mediocre."

Manwhile I discovered that women advisees were as capable of taking over one's lectures and repeating them as their own as men. If anything, they made the discovery more quickly than men, that one could conceal indebtedness while presumably acknowledging it, but burying the acknowledgement of genuine help in a garland of spurious acknowledgements. Finally, in the instant they obtained their degrees, women (some, of course, not all) often terminated all further friendly exchange more quickly than men—almost as if in pique at the failure of an advisor to accept an invitation to dance at the time he had the chance.

Someday when the sociology of advising is explored in depth, the consequences of love affairs between advisors and advisees may be examined in detail: be they heterosexual affairs between male advisors and female students and female advisors and male students or homosexual affairs between two men or two women across the advisor-advisee relationship. I rather suspect that it will be discovered that, although the hetero—or homosexual love affair is often personally and professionally disastrous in the lives of advisors and advisees, that for a time it heats the advisor-advisee relationship to incandescence and the advisor never before imparted so much information or with so much imagination and the advisee never before learned so much or was so completely lifted to a higher plane of insight and understanding.

Notes

1. Elbridge Sibley, *The Education of Sociologists in the United States* (New York: Russell Sage Foundation, 1963), p. 51.

2. Jessie Bernard, *Academic Women* (University Park: The Pennsylvania State University Press, 1964).

3. Juanita M. Kreps, "Sex and the Scholarly Girl," American Association of University Professors *Bulletin* 51 (1) (March 1965), p. 32.

4. E. Scott, "Statistical Data for Academic Women at Berkeley." Unpublished (University of California, Berkeley, 1969).

5. L. Seigel, "The Contributions and Implications of Recent Research Research Related to Improving Teaching and Learning." In M. Ohmer and J. Shobern, *Learning the Professor* (3rd ed.; Athens, Ohio: Ohio University Press, 1968).

6. Ann M. Heiss, *Challenges to Graduate Schools: The Ph.D. Program in Ten Universities* (San Francisco: Jossey-Bass, 1970), p. 95.

7. See also P. A. Heist, "Intellect and Commitment: The Faces of Discontent." In O. A. Knorr and W. J. Minter (eds.), *Order and Freedom on the Campus*. Western Interstate Commission for Higher Education and Center for Research and Development in Higher Education (Berkeley, 1965).

8. *Fact Book on Higher Education*. American Council on Education, 1976, 75:197.

9. One of my own male advisees who was also my teaching assistant, for example, came to me with the story of how one sophisticated girl in my class, who was of some special interest to me for she was the daughter of one of my own former teachers many years before at the University of Wisconsin, had bragged to mutual friends that she intended to "make the T. A. in Martindale's course before the end of the quarter." Since it had long been my policy not to inquire into the personal lives of my advisees, I never asked him whether she succeeded. However, it occurred to me at the time I heard this incident—which incidentally was related to me by my T.A. with tones of sophistication, humor, and flattered vanity that would have done credit to Groucho Marx—such are the wiles of the feminine strategy, that the boast might have been deliberately made to mutual friends

of herself and the T.A. with the intention that it get back to him and serve as an invitation to intimacy and a self-fulfilling prophecy. The message was: "Well, now you know. If you are interested the rest is up to you."

10. Marianne Weber, *Max Weber: A Biography.* Tr. Harry Sohn (New York: John Wiley & Sons, 1975), p. 373.

11. Ibid., p. 387.

12. Ibid., p. 388.

13. Don Martindale, *The Romance of a Profession* (St. Paul. Minn.: Windflower, 1976), pp. 156–163.

14. Adrienne Munich, "Seduction in Academe," *Psychology Today,* February, 1978, pp. 82–84, 108.

15. Letters to the Editor, *Psychology Today,* May, 1978, p. 18.

16. *Ibid.,* p. 18.

17. Munich, ',Seduction in Academe," p. 108.

APPENDIX: STATISTICS ON DOCTORAL ADVISING IN SOCIOLOGY AT THE UNIVERSITY OF MINNESOTA

In the history of the Minnesota sociology department, the major growth of its graduate program occurred in the period following World War II. The total number of persons earning the doctor's degree in sociology at Minnesota as of June, 1977 was 277. From 1900 to 1950 a total of 40 doctoral degrees in sociology were granted at Minnesota. Only one less than this, 39, were granted in the next decade alone.

Sociology Ph.D.'s at the University of
Minnesota by Decade:
1900 to June 1977

Time Period	Number of Doctoral Degrees Granted in Sociology
Prior to 1920	2
1920–1929	11
1930–1939	19
1940–1949	8
1950–1959	39
1960–1969	89
1970–June 1977	109
Total	277

Two persons received doctoral degrees in sociology at Minnesota even before the university acquired an organized doctoral program under the guidance of F. Stuart Chapin in 1922. Once the graduate program was organized in the

1920s the production of Ph.D.'s increased and 11 persons earned the doctoral degree in sociology between 1922 and 1929. Despite the economic depression in the 1930s the number of doctoral degrees was almost doubled. The effect of World War II in the 1940s was manifest in the sharp drop in the number of doctoral degrees awarded. Through the entire period of his chairmanship F. Stuart Chapin was the most popular doctoral advisor. Of the 38 degrees awarded in Sociology at the University of Minnesota between 1922 and 1949 nearly three-fourths, 27 of them were under the direction or codirection of Chapin. He was to put through 5 more in his last two years after giving up the chairmanship.

Expansion of the graduate program in the 1950s at Minnesota as at other major universities of the United States was inevitable for a number of reasons: (1) there was a backlog of graduate students whose academic careers had been delayed by military service; (2) many of these students had G. I. benefits which would help finance their degree programs; (3) it was a period of affluence and of expanding demand for social scientists.

One effect of the expansion of the graduate program at Minnesota in the post war period, was to terminate the possibility that doctoral advising could remain largely a one man show. This may be seen by the distribution of advisors with five or more persons who earned the Ph.D. under their direction at Minnesota in the period from 1902 when the first Ph.D. was awarded in Sociology through June of 1977.

Numbers of Ph.D.s by Sociology Professor at the University of Minnesota: 1902 to June 1977

Professor*	Number of Ph.D.s
Don Martindale	73
F. Stuart Chapin	32
Arnold Rose	16
Reuben Hill	14
Elio D. Monachesi	12
R. G. Francis and Gregory P. Stone, each	11
Lowry Nelson	9
Malcolm Willey	7
David Cooperman, George Donohue, C. E. Ramsey, I. Reiss, M. Taves and George Vold, each	5

* Professors with less than five not included. The increase in the production of Ph.D.s at Minnesota is parallel to that in the United States as a whole. In the period 1947–48, there were 66 sociology doctoral degrees awarded in the United States; in 1973–74, 632 were awarded.

When the American Sociological Association compiled the data for its 1976 Guide to Graduate Departments of Sociology, a questionnaire was sent to all known graduate departments in the United States and Canada (N=282). Eventually replies were received from 225 graduate sociology departments: 209 American departments, 16 Canadian departments.

In the United States 115 of the 209 responding departments listed the offer of both M.A. and Ph.D. degrees (94 offered the M.A. or M.S. only). In Canada 5 out of the 16 departments listed both M.A. and Ph.D. programs (11 offer the M.A. only), At least 120 departments in the United States and Canada offered the doctorate in sociology.

Don Martindale's Ph.D.'s by Date and Topic

Date	Name	Dissertation Topic
1955	Richard Emerson	Submission to Social Influence in Face-to-Face Groups
1958	Seymour Leventman	Class and Ethnic Tensions: The Stratification of a Minority Group
1958	Judith Kramer	Fathers and Sons: Conflict Resolutions of Third Generation American Jews
1960	Roger G. Krohn	Science and Social Change: The Effects of New Institutional Locals on the Traditional Structure of Science
1960	Leonard Weller	The Nature of Prejudice: A Theoretical Evaluation and an Empirical Appraisal
1960	Keith A. Lovald	From Hobohemia to Skid Row: The Changing Community of the Homeless Man
1961	Clarence Dale Johnson	Priest, Prophet, and Professional Man: A Study of Religious Leadership in a Small Community
1961	Alex Simirenko	Pilgrims, Colonists and Frontiersmen: An Ethnic Community in Transition
1962	Mary Adams	Functionalism versus Social Behaviorism in the Current Sociology of Illness: A Test of the Empirical Adequacy of Theory

Date	Name	Dissertation Topic
1963	Noel Iverson	Germania, U.S.A.: The Dynamics of Change of an Ethic Community into a Status Community
1963	Nicos Mouratides	Psychiatrists in the Mental Hospital: A Study in Role Tensions and Conflict
1963	Santosh Kumar Nandy	The Traditional and the Modern in the Idea of Social Change in Post-independence India
1963	Ira E. Robinson	Basic and Improving Inventions in Industry: A Study of the Research Scientists of Minneapolis-Honeywell
1964	Ronald Althouse	The Intellectual Career of F. Stuart Chapin: An Examination of the Development and Contributions of a Pluralistic Behaviorist
1964	Alvin Boderman	Feelings of Powerlessness and Political and Religious Extremism
1964	Perry E. Jacobson, Jr.	The Dynamics of Inter-faith Marriages
1964	Thomas Philbrook	Industrialization in the Small Community: A Study of Three Newfoundland Communities
1964	Jack Cole Ross	Traditionalism and Charisma in a Religious Group: Membership, Careers and Role Contingencies of Quakers

Date	Name	Dissertation Topic
1964	Robert A. Stebbins	The Jazz Community: The Sociology of a Musical Sub-Culture
1965	Thomas E. Carroll	How the Punishment Fits the Crime: The Criteria of Sentencing Used by Criminal Court Judges in Dade County, Florida
1966	Tai Shick Kang	Identity and Assimilation: The Study of a Foreign Student Colony
1966	Myrtle Korenbaum	Role Cacophony: The Source of Tension in Role Enactment, A Study of University and College Professors
1967	Rajnikant S. Gandhi	Little India: Localism and Cosmopolitanism in an Indian Student Colony
1967	Russell Galen Hanson	The Crisis of Benson: A Small Town Orients to the Mass Society
1967	Yoon Hough Kim	The Community of the Blind; A Test Case for Application of the Theory of Community Formation
1967	Robert P. Snow	Institutional Centralization and Communal Particularism: A Study of Role Tensions of Public Health Nurses
1968	Robindra C. Chakravorti	The Sikhs of El Centro: A Study of Social Integration

Date	Name	Dissertation Topic
1968	Robert Gliner	A Comparison of French and American Avant-Garde Literature: A Study in the Sociology of Knowledge
1968	Mohamed Ezzat Hegazy	Cross-cultural Experience and Social Change: The Case of Foreign Study
1968	Robert J. Lazar	From Ethnic Minority to Socio-economic Elite: A Study of the Jewish Community of Fargo, North Dakota
1968	Proshanta Kumar Nandi	Career and Life Organization of Professionals: A Study of Contrasts Between College and University Professors
1968	Ramon Almich Oldenburg	Companionship and Identity as Reflected in Marital Leisure Patterns
1968	Charlotte Wolf	The Garrison Community: A Study of an Overseas American Military Colony
1968	Mathew Zachariah	Wither Kerala? Social Change in Twentieth Century Kerala
1969	Arnold Dashefsky	Social Interaction and Jewish Self-Conception: A Two Generation Analysis of the St. Paul Community
1969	R. Frank Falk	Self Concept and Mobility Aspiration: A Study of Changing Self Definitions of Teacher Aides
1969	William James Geer	The Artist as a Member of a Formal Organization

Date	Name	Dissertation Topic
1969	Thomas M. Kando	The Social Consequences of Sex Achievement: A Study of the Social Relations of Fifteen Transsexuals After Their Conversion Operation
1969	Edward Charles Knop	Timbertown in Transition: Perspectives on Community Formation, Maintenance and Decline
1969	John Ailen Landsverk	The Impact of Religious Affiliation on Secular Aspiration and Achievement Among Minnesota Public High School Students
1969	Harvey James Lally	Competition and Violence in the American Character
1969	Howard M. Shapiro	Marginality, Familial Interaction, and Intellectuality: The Shaping of Perspective in a Jewish Community
1969	C. Edwin Vaughn	An Empirical Study of the Relationship between Participation in University Extracurricular Activities and Student Alienation
1969	Richard W. Wunderlich	Institutional Context and the Scientific Tradition
1970	Rita Braito	Conflict Legitimation and Forms of Protest
1970	Joan Gerads	Health Needs in the Parroquia de San Bartolome
1970	Ronald O. Haverlandt	Religion and Social Change: The American Churches and the Anti-war Movement, 1960–1970

Date	Name	Dissertation Topic
1970	Donald G. Herron	Alienation and Student Orientation in the Contemporary University
1970	D. Ralph Matthews	Communities in Transition: An Examination of Government Initiated Community Migration in Rural Newfoundland
1970	Amos O. Odenyo	Africans and Afro-Americans on Campus: A Study of Some of the Relationships Between Two Minority Sub-Communities
1970	Musab U. Siddiqi	Parental Participation in the Sex Education Program: An Evaluative Study
1970	Frithjof O. M. Westby	The Blue-collar Worker: A Study of Socio-cultural Influences on Work Behavior
1971	Penny Hiatt Baron	Effects of Self-Esteem and Evaluation Instructions on Evaluations of Self and Others
1971	Raymond J. Cummings	AFDC Caseworker Social Value Orientations and the Employment Outcome of AFDC Clients
1971	William Roy DeMaree, Jr.	Marginality in the Paraprofessional: A Study of the Graduate Teaching Assistant as Marginal Man
1971	Juanita Ann Nada Dobmeyer	The Sociology of Shoplifting: Avocation and Vocation
1971	Margaret-Mary Franz	Social Alienation, Self Alienation and Group Membership

Date	Name	Dissertation Topic
1971	George Russell Hatton	The Crisis of Minto
1971	Samiha Sidhom Peterson	Elites and the Modernization of Underdeveloped Countries: The Case of Egypt
1971	Alex G. Stach	Hippie Communes U.S.A.: Five Case Studies, 1970
1972	Rong-Rong Lo	Marriage Patterns and Modernization in Taiwan
1972	Jai P. Ryu	From Chosen to Daehan: Social Change in Twentieth Century Korea
1972	George W. Stevenson	Social Control in Institutions of Higher Educatio: Administration Responses to Student Protest at the University of Minnesota and Macalester College (1967/1972)
1973	Wallace H. Hustad	The Paradox of Suburbanization
1973	Patricia Anne Hartman	Social Variation in Magical Belief
1974	Henry C. Chang	Library Goals as Responses to Structural and Milieu Requirements: A Comparative Case Study
1974	Robert Earl Franz, Jr.	Social Psychological Factors Influencing Success in Job Training

Date	Name	Dissertation Topic
1974	Harold Leonard Orbach	The Disengagement Theory of Aging, 1960-1970: A Case Study of Scientific Controversy
1974	Sister Marlene Weber, FSPA	The Role of Religion in Society: A Study of Patterns in a Religious-affiliated College and a State University
1974	Arthur S. Wilke	Youthfulness as a Product of the Social Changes Accompanying the Rise of Mass Society
1975	Viviane Doche	A Generational Study of Assimilation Among the Lebanese in the Twin Cities
1975	Judith Unteregger-Mattenberger	The Roots of a Social Movement: An Exploratory Study of Women's Self-conceptions and Changing Sex Roles in Switzerland
1975	Mary Catherine Schroepfer	Disabilities in the Elderly

BIBLIOGRAPHY

Alciatore, R. T. and Eckert, R. *Minnesota Ph.D.'s Evaluate Their Training*. Minneapolis: University of Minnesota Press, 1968.

Althouse, Ronald. "The Intellectual Career of F. Stuart Chapin: An Examination of the Contribution of a Pluralistic Behaviorist." Unpublished doctoral dissertation, University of Minnesota, 1964. Pp. 142-146. Review of Chapin as a graduate advisor, pp. 142-146.

Axelrod, J. (ed.). *Graduate Study for Future College Teachers*. Washington, D. C.: American Council on Education, 1959.

Barzun, J. *Graduate Study at Columbia*. New York: Columbia University Press, 1958.

Berelson, Bernard. *Graduate Education in the United States*. New York: McGraw-Hill, 1960.

Bernard, J. *Academic Women*. University Park, Pa.: Pennsylvania State University Press, 1964.

Bradwish, Sharon Lee. "George Bryan Vold: The Intellectual Biography of a Conflict Theorist." Unpublished M.A. thesis, University of Minnesota, 1967. Vold as a Ph.D. advisor, pp. 63-66.

Caplow, T. and McGee, R. J. *The Academic Market Place*. New York: Basic Books, 1959.

Carmichael, O. C. *Graduate Education: A Critique and a Program*. New York: Harper & Row, 1961.

Carter, A. M. *An Assessment of Quality in Graduate Education*. Washington, D. C: American Council on Education, 1966.

_____. "Discussion of the Berelson Heresy." In *Doctoral Programs in Small Liberal Arts Colleges.* Symposium at Bowdoin College, Brunswick, Maine, April 1967.

Committee of Fifteen. *The Graduate School Today and Tomorrow: Reflections for the Profession's Consideration.* New York: Fund for the Advancement of Education, 1955.

Craig, C. M. *Graduate Education.* New York: Center for Applied Research in Education, Inc., 1965.

David, J. A. *Great Aspirations.* Chicago: Aldine, 1964.

Devane, W. C. *Higher Education in Twentieth-Century America.* Cambridge: Harvard University Press, 1965.

Eurich, A. C., Kenney, L. B. and Tickton, S. G. *The Expansion of Graduate Education During the Period 1966 to 1980.* Studies in the Future of Higher Education, Report No. 2. New York: The Academy for Educational Development, April 1969.

Gottlieb, D. "Process of Socialization in American Graduate Schools." Unpublished doctoral dissertation, University of Chicago, 1960.

_____. "American Graduate Students: Some Characteristics of Aspiring Teachers and Researchers," *Journal of Educational Psychology,* 52 (5) (1961), 236-240.

Gropper, G. L. and Fitzpatrick, R. *Who Goes to Graduate School?* Pittsburgh, Pa.: American Institute for Research, 1959.

Heard, A. *The Lost Years in Graduate Education.* Atlanta, Ga.: Southern Regional Education Board, 1963.

Heiss, A. M. "Berkeley Doctoral Students Appraise Their Academic Programs," *The Educational Record* (Winter 1967), 30-44.

_____. "Graduate Education Today: An Instrument of Change ? *Journal of Higher Education,* 34 (January 1968).

_____. *Challenges to Graduate Schools.* San Francisco: Jossey-Bass, 1970.

Heyns, R. W. "The Graduate Students: Teacher, Research Assistant, or Scholar ?" *The Graduate Journal,* XII (2) (1967), 310.

Horton, B. J. *The Graduate School.* New York: New York University Book Store, 1940.

James, W. "The Ph.D. Octopus." In *Memories and Studies.* New York: Longmans Green. 1911.

Jencks, C. and Riesman, D. *The Academic Revolution.* Garden City, New York: Doubleday, 1968.

Johnson, R. C. "Reflections on the Ph.D.," *College English,* 26 (4) (1965), 304-306.

Keniston, H. J. *Graduate Study and Research in the Arts and Sciences at the University of Pennsylvania.* Philadelphia, Pa: University of Pennsylvania Press, 1959.

Kent, L. J. and Spring, G. P. (eds.). *Graduate Education Today and Tomorrow.* Albuquerque: University of New Mexico Press, 1972.

Kerr, C. *The Uses of the University.* Cambridge: Harvard University Press, 1963.

Kreps, J. M. "Sex and the Scholarly Girl." American Association of University Professors *Bulletin,* 51 (1) (March 1965), 30-33.

Martindale, Don. *The Romance of a Profession.* St. Paul, Minn.: Windflower Publishing Co., 1976.

Mayhew, L. B. *Graduate and Professional Education, 1980.* New York: McGraw Hill, 1970.

McGrath, E. *The Graduate School and the Decline of Liberal Education.* New York: Teachers College, Columbia University, 1959.

Miller, J. P. "The Graduate School in the University Community," *Ventures,* VI (1) (1966), 1-4.

National Science Board. *Graduate Education: Parameters for Public Policy.* Washington, D. C.: U. S. Government Printing Office, 1969.

National Science Foundation. *Graduate Student Support and Manpower Resources in Graduate Science Education.* (Fall 1965; Fall 1968). NSF 63-13. Washington, D. C: U. S. Government Printing Office, June 1968.

Ness, F. and James, B. *Graduate Study in the Liberal Arts College.* Washington, D. C,: Commission on Professional and Graduate Study, Association of American Colleges, 1962.

Nicholas, R. T. "Administering Graduate Schools." In E. Walters (ed.), *Graduate Education.* Washington, D.C.: American Council of Education, 1965.

_____. "A Reconsideration of the Ph.D.," *The Graduate Journal,* 12 (2) (1967), 325-335.

Nowlis, V. *et al , The Graduate Student as Teacher.* Washington, D. C.: American Council on Education, Education Monograph, 1968.

Putman, F. W. "Toward a Public Policy for Graduate Education in the Sciences," *Science,* 163 (1969), 1147.

Quick, R. *A Guide to Graduate Study.* Fourth Edition; Washington, D. C.: American Council on Education, 1969.

Reisman, D. *Constraint and Variety in American Education.* New York: Doubleday, 1958.

Rogers, C. R. *Graduate Education in Psychology: A Passionate Statement.* La Jolla, Calif.: Western Institute of Behavioral Science, 1964.

Rosenhaupt, H. *Graduate Students: Experiences at Columbia University, 1940-1956.* New York: Columbia University Press, 1956.

Sanford, N. (ed.) *The American College: A Psychological and Sociological Interpretation of Higher Learning.* New York: Wiley, 1962.

Sawyer, R. A. "The Graduate Student and the University Research Program," *The Graduate Journal,* 7 (2) (1954). 317.

Sharp, L. M. "Graduate Study and Its Relation to Careers: The Experience of a Recent Cohort of College Graduates," *Human Resources,* 1 (1966), 41-58.

_____. *Education and Employment: The Early Careers of College Graduates.* Baltimore: The Johns Hopkins Press, 1970.

Sibley, Elbridge. *The Education of Sociologists in the United States.* Washington, D. C.: Russell Sage Foundation, 1963.

Snyder, P. O. *Graduate and Professional Opportunities for Minority Students in the West.* Boulder, Colo.: Western Interstate Commission for Higher Education, August 1969.

Sorokin, Pitirim A. *A Long Journey: The Autobiography of Pitirim A. Sorokin.* Some notes on Sorokin's activities as teacher and advisor at Harvard appear in the section "The Story of the Department," pp. 247-251.

Spurr, S. H. *Degree Structures in American Higher Education.* New York: McGraw-Hill, 1970.

Stanford University. *Graduate Education.* Report to the University Steering Committee of the Study of Education at Stanford, VIII (1968-1969).

Veblen, T. *The Higher Learning in America.* New York: Hill and Wang, 1965.

Walters, E. (ed.). *Graduate Education Today.* Washington, D. C.: American Council on Education, 1965.

West, A. *The Graduate College of Princeton.* Princeton: Princeton University Press, 1913.

Wilson, Kenneth W. *Of Time and the Doctorate.* SREB Research Monograph, N. 9. Atlanta: Southern Regional Education Board, 1965.

INDEX

Adams, Mary, 190
Adelson, Joseph, 2-4, 21, 24
Adler, Mortimer, 8-9
advisees, doctoral:
    appointed, 35-36
    choice of advisor, 29-31
    colleagues, 102-117
    exploitation of advisors, 30-31, 116-117
    identification with advisors, 124-126
    satisfaction with advisors, 2, 22-23, 70
advising policy, 40-48
advisors, doctoral :
    attitudes toward advisees, 102-103
    exploitation of advisees, 31, 111-113
    graduate student attitudes toward, 22-23
    types, 2-5, 21-23
    women advisees of, 161-186
Agard, Walter, 5, 22, 24
Alice in Wonderland, 13
Althouse, Ronald, 191
Alliance Against Sexual Coercion, 177
Army, U. S., 168-170
Augsburg College, 98

Bachmann, Solomon, 31-32, 38-40
Barnes, Harry Elmer, 12
Baron, Penny Hiatt, 195
Becker, Howard P., 5, 12-13, 14, 15-18, 19, 22, 27-29, 31, 38, 50, 65-67, 83, 89, 171
Becker, Howard S., 128
Benedict, Ruth, iii-iv, v

Berelson, B., 36, 49, 83, 117
Bernard, Jessie, 161–162, 185
Berkeley, University, 23
Blumer, Herbert, 128
Bode, Carl, 133
Boderman, Alvin, 191
Braito, Rita, 194
Bureau of Applied Social Research, 32–33, 36, 40

Calgary (University of), 158
California (University of), 23
call girls, 172
Capitalists Without Capitalism, 98
Caplow, Theodore, 64
Carroll. Thomas E., 192
Chakravorti, Robindra C , 192
Challenge to the Graduate Schools, 23, 24
Chang, Henry C., 196
Chapin, F. Stuart, 30–31, 33, 45, 48, 61, 64, 121–122, 187, 188, 189
Character and Social Structure, 39, 40
Chicago (University of), 8, 15, 65, 105
Columbia University, 23, 32–33, 39, 173–174
Colvard, Richard, 129
companionate marriage, 165–177
Cooperman, David, 189
Cornell University, 23, 177
Cumings, Raymond J. 195

Dashevsky, Arnold, 193
DeMaree, William Roy, 195
Department of Justice, Federal, 177
Dewey, John, 8, 67–69, 83
Dickson, W. J., 17
dissertation myths, 69–74

Dobmeyer, Juanita, Ann Nada, 195
Donohue, Geeorge, 128, 189
Dreiser, Theodore, 166

Educational Ammendments Act, 175
Ellenbogen, Bert, 128
Emerson, Richard Marc, 119–120, 190
Ernest, William, 140–159
Experimental College (of U. of Wisconsin), 6-7, 24

Falk, R. Frank, 193
Fiske, John, 62
Floro, George K., 124
Francis, Roy G., 34, 189
Frank, Glenn, 6, 24
Franz, Margaret-Mary, 195
Franz, Robert Earl, Jr., 196
Freud, Sigmund, 165
From Max Weber, 39, 49
Fulton, Robert, 128
funded research (influence on advising relationship), 41–42

Gandhi, Rajnikant S., 192
Garfinkel, Harold, 180
Geer, William James, 193
Gerth, Hans, 6, 13, 18–20, 21, 28, 38–40, 43, 49, 94, 136–138, 142, 171, 172
G. I. student aid, 59–60, 90
Gliner, Robert, 193
Goffman, Erving, 128
Goodnight, Dean Scott, H., 167
Graduate Education in the United States, 36, 49, 117
graduate students :
    attrition, 87–89
    drop outs, 86–88
    teaching assistants, 53–54

INDEX

types, 58–61
women, 62–63
Grahame, Kenneth, 13
Goldenweiser, Alexander, iii–iv
Gross, Neal, 64
Gustavus Adolphus College, 97

Hagstrom, Warren O., 117, 119–134
Hanson, Russell Galen, 192
Hartman, Patricia Anne, 196
Hatton, George Russell, 196
Haverlandt, Ronald O., 194
Heath, D. C. and Company, 28–29, 43
Hagezy, Mohamed Ezzat, 193
Heiss, Ann, 22–23, 24, 25, 37, 49, 70, 73, 84, 87, 91, 100, 159, 185
Hemmingway, Ernest, 166
Herron, Donad G., 195
Hill, Reuben, 128, 189
Hutchins, Robert, 8
Hook, Sidney, 8
Hustad, Wallace H., 196
Huxley, Aldous, 166

ideal types (constructs), 14–15
Ingraham, Mark H., 17
Iowa (University of), 10
Iverson, Noel, 191

Jackson, Merrill, 2–3
Jacobson, Perry E. Jr., 191
James, William 8, 69, 84
Johns Hopkins University, 23
Johnson, C. Dale, 48, 104, 190

Kando, Thomas M., 194
Kang, Tai Shick, 192

Karve, Dr. Irawati, 97–98
Kirkpatrick, Clifford, 30, 64
Kim, Yoon Hough, 192
Klotz, M. See Max Otto, 7
Knop, Edward C., 194
Korean War, 173
Korenbaum, Myrtle, 50, 192
Kovacs, Maria, 181
Kramer, Judith, 190
Kreps, Juanita, 185
Krohn, Roger, 84–49, 190

Lally, Harvey James, 194
Landsverk, John Allen, 194
Lawrence, D. H., 166, 168
laboratory experiments in sociology, 119–120
Laird, Arthur, 24
Lazar, Robert J., 193
Leonard, William Ellery, 54–55, 167
Leventman, Seymour, 190
Lo (Mrs. Yang), Rong-Rong, 196
Logic : The Theory of Enquiry, 67–69, 83
Lovald, Kieth A., 190
Lundberg, George, 121

Malinowski, Bronislaw, iv–v
Manheim, Karl, 20
Marshall, Douglas, 64
Martindale, Don, 29, 46, 48, 51, 100, 113, 115, 116, 117, 123, 127, 128, 130, 179, 185, 189
Marxism, 8
Mathew Effect in Science, 27, 48
Matthews, D. Ralph, 195
Milkejohn, Alexander, 24
Memorial University of Newfoundland, 99

Merton, Robert K., 27, 48
Michelangelo, 3
Michigan (University of), 23
Mickelson, Harland S., 119
Mills, C. Wright, 13, 14, 38–40, 49, 50, 106, 127, 172
Milton, John, 154–156
Minnesota Department of Corrections, 99
Minnesota (University of), 28, 29, 34, 86, 96, 121, 128, 130, 173, 187–197
Monachesi, Elio D., 48, 64, 189
Mouratides, Nicos, 191
Munich, Adrienne, 175, 176, 177, 178, 180, 181, 185
myths, graduate student, 70–74
McCormick, T. C., 6, 14, 18, 19, 43, 171

Nandi, Proshanta Kumar, 193
Nandy, Santosh Kumar, 191
National Science Foundation, 62
Nature and Types of Sociological Theory, 121
Nelson, Lowry, 30, 64, 189
Nevaskar, Balwant, 96–98
Nietzsche, F., 183
New England Conservatory of Music, 178

Odenyo, Amos O., 195
Ogburn, William, 15
Old World Traits Transplanted, 114
Oldenburg, Ramon A., 193
Orbach, Harold Leonard, 197
Oregon (University of), 157
Otto, Max, 7–8, 10, 12, 24, 25, 166
Oxford University Press, 38

Park, Robert, 15, 65, 114
Patterns of Culture, iv
Peterson, Samiha Sidhom, 196

Peck, Louise, 136-137, 142
Peck, Sidney, 136-137, 142
Pennsylvania State College, 178
Perlman, Selig, 18-19
Ph. D., i-iv, 22-23, 62-63, 70-74, 86f, 89, 102f, 112, 161, 162, 187-197
Philbrook, Thomas, 191
Poona (University of), 97
Power Elite, 39, 40
Price, Pamela, 178
Pride, Charles, 140-159
Professors :
    career stages, 107-109
    mid-life crisis, 108
prostitutes, 169, 172
Proust, M., 166
Puget Sound (University of), 98

Quackenbush, Orville, 138-140, 142
Quijada, Alonzo See Eliseo Vivas, 7

Radcliffe College, 177
Ramsey, C. Eugene, 128, 189
Redfield, Robert, 83
Reiss, Ira, 189
retread, 177-178
Rickson, Roy, 157-159
Robinson, Ira E., 191
Rocking Chair Incident, 167
Roethlisberger, F. J., 17
Rogers, C. R., 100
Romance of a Profession, 48, 51, 99, 100, 121-133, 185
Rose, Arnold, 64, 104-105, 106, 130, 189
Ross, Jack Cole, 191
Ryu, Jai P., 196

Sanford, Nevitt, 24
Schroepfer, Mary Catherine, 192
scientific problems, Dewey on, 67–69
Scott, E. 185
"Seduction in Academe," 175, 185
Seifert, Joyce, 178
Seigel, L., 185
Sellery, George Clark, 55–57
Sex Exchange Monitoring System, 175
sexual harassment, 50–51, 172–173, 175f
sex mores :
    revolution in 164f
Sharp, Laure, 36, 49, 61, 62, 74, 83, 84, 159
Shapiro, Howard M., 194
Sherif, Muzafer, 120
Shibutani, Tomatsu, 128
Sibley, Elbridge, 62, 83, 86, 100, 161, 185
Siddiqi, Musab, 195
Simirenko, Alex, 190
Simmel, Georg, 14, 65
Sirjamaki, John, 114–115
Sjoberg, Gideon, 129
Snow, Robert P., 192
Social Thought from Lore to Science, 12–13
sociology :
    Canada, graduate departments, 189
    Minnesota, 121–123, 130–131
    United States, graduate departments, 189
Sorokin, Pitirim A., 121
Stach, Alex G., 196
Stanford University, 23
Stebbins, Robert A., 192
Stern, Lawrence, 10
Stevenson, George W., 196

Stone, Gregory P., 189
Straus, Anselm, 128
Sutherland, Edwin, 121
symbolic interactionism, 128, 130

Taves, Marvin, 189
teachers, 2–5, 21–22
teaching assistants, 53–54
Thoreau, Henry David, 133
Timper, Pricilla, 124, 131, 134
Tobias, Sheila, 182
Tucker, A., 88, 100
Twain, Mark, 131

Unteregger-Mattenberger, Judith, 197

Vaughn, C. Edwin, 194
Victorianism, 166f
Vivas, Eliseo, 5, 7–12, 22, 24, 25, 166
Vold, George, 120, 138–139, 142, 189

Washington (University of), 159
Weber, Marianne, 164–165, 185
Weber, Max, 15, 38–39, 165
Weber, Sister Marlene, 197
Weinberg, S. K., 130
Weller, Leonard, 190
Westby, Frithjof O. M., 195
White Collar, 39, 40
Wiese, Leopold von, 12
Wilke, Arthur, 197
Willey, Malcolm, 189
Williams, Diane, 177
Wind in the Willows, 13
Wirth, Louis, 104–105
Wisconsin Sociologist, 122–133

Wisconsin (University of), 5-15, 16, 17-18, 19, 23, 24, 27, 53, 107, 128, 136, 167, 170
Wolf, Charlotte, 193
women :
    academic opportunities, 161-163
    advisees, 163-164
    sexual harassment, 50-51, 171-184
    types, 163-164
Working Women's United Institute, 177
World War II, 5, 15, 38, 187
Wunderlich, Richard W., 194

Yale University, 175f, 178

Zachariah, Mathew, 193
Zimmerman, Carle C., 121
Zwerman, William, 157-159

Viscusi, W. (Kip) (Liebow, Jr.), 2–14, 16, 17–19, 19, 20, 24, 27, 107, 130, 136, 166, 170
Wolf, Charlotte, 123
women:
and hiring opportunities, 151–152
and wages, 137–151
sexual harassment, 89–91, 178–184
types, 152–164
Working Women United Institute, 179
World War II, 6, 18, 30, 167
Wuesthoff, Richard W., 94

Yale University, 124, 176

Zalaznick, Matthew, 180
Zimmerman, Carle C., 121
Zwerman, William, 137–139